ENOUGH:
Unlock a life of abundance
starting right where you are

ENOUGH:
Unlock your life of abundance starting right where you are

First published in November 2021

The Right Company Press

ISBN 978-0-6453399-1-8 (Ebook)

ISBN 978-0-6453399-0-1 (Paperback)

Editor: Jeremy Deedes

Contributors: Ian Berry, Claudia Brose, Con Christesen, Jacqueline Davis, Jeremy Deedes, Mark Dyck, Caroline Harvey, Sue Heatherington, Joel Hughes, Jacquie Landeman, Kim LeClair, Darcy Lee, Pete Michaels, Cat Preston, Ulla Raaf, Tricia Van Vleit.

Design: Ulla Raaf, www.ullaraaf.com

"If people interest you, and the distilled wisdom of peoples' experiences fascinate you, then you will cherish this collection."
Terry McGivern, Regional Managing Director (CEER ME APAC)
Kingspan light +Air, Cavan, Ireland

"A wonderful and vital compendium of inspirational thoughts and ideas for living a more fulfilled life. Incredibly empowering to help you ensure you don't die with your music locked inside you."
John F Kennedy BSc FIDM PG DipDM, United Kingdom

"Ian teachings, stories and words ring true to me as life lived experiences and he brings clearness, understanding and direction to all who know him. All collaboration Ian is involved in must mean a wonderful bunch of people have been engaged in this project."
Jamie Wilson, Regional Sales Manager, Australia

"I have bookshelves lined with books that I have read once, and I have one special shelf that holds my 'go to' books. The 'go to' books have the feeling that is an odd mixture of inspiration, wisdom, challenges and comfortable slippers.
Enough belongs on the 'go to' shelf, it has how to start journey's, how to learn from miss-steps (there is no such thing as a mistake) it has reasons why and it has friendships that can be leaned into."
Rosemary McKenzie-Ferguson, Founder Craig's Table, Recipient
2021 Comp Laude Humanitarian Award, Australia

"Book shops and libraries are full of self-help volumes for people in business who may be frustrated and who desire to change and improve their situation. Why this book then? Enough, is different in that it features sixteen diverse first-person accounts of how experienced managers and entrepreneurs from many different parts of the world have successfully confronted these very issues and transformed their professional lives. It is not a book which offers a single formula or strategy but, rather, provides different real-life examples and, hopefully inspiration, on how to move forward on your own unique path. You will be informed and also entertained. I highly recommend this book to anyone looking to blaze their own trail but who might be having some difficulty defining the way."

John McDermott, internationally recognized photographer and writer, USA/Italy

"ENOUGH is a wonderful collection of stories and insights that will help you see yourself afresh. You'll encounter a cadre of beautiful humans you would love to ponder life over a drink with. They'll ask probing questions and invite you in practical ways to step further into the life you're seeking. Each section offers a new angle on how you can do work that's both meaningful and joy-filled at the same time."

Lon Wong, change agent, social entrepreneur and author of 'Dear Stellar: Letters on the art of being human', Canada

„*This was a heartwarming read filled with diverse mix of creativity, inspiration, and stories that warmed my heart, and moved my soul. I enjoyed the practical wisdom as well as the creative inspiration I found within each story and journey shared. I had an certain idea of what the word Enough meant, but after reading the book, my idea and concepts of all that the word enough holds has expanded greatly. I loved the digital version AND I'm excited to get my hard copy soon.*"
Enrika Greathouse, Small Gorilla Creative Marketing, USA

"*Do we just keep doing what we've been doing or do we want to try something new this time? These stories from wonderful people around the globe are all real, intense and personal. Let them take you away and inspire you to make your own next steps.*"
Michael Wahrheit, Wahrheit Design, Germany

Enough forms an assembly of wise souls and trusted mentors, distilling their best advice into a powerful call-to-action. It combines practical tips and compelling stories, forming a beautifully paced piece of work. Enough reassures that your own unique talents and perspective mean you already have the tools you need to curate the life you want. It then gently takes you by the hand and says, "now let's try this…" Think of Enough as a user guide for creatives – especially those who feel stuck, rudderless or weighed down with imposter syndrome. It swerves well-worn platitudes and instead presents a generous edit of new ideas, habits and ways of working. It's a book that's as hopeful as it is wise.
Fiona Mattesini, journalist and writer, UK

Content

About Mark Dyck

Mark Dyck is a writer, podcaster, coach and community leader and is the Chief Community Advocate for *the Right Company.* He lives in Victoria, BC, Canada.

Meet Mark at:
https://markdyck.co
http://riseuppod.com
https://linkedin.com/in/markdyck

Foreword

Mark Dyck (Canada)

When Bernadette and I launched the Right Company in 2018, we didn't know what to expect. All we knew was that, through her blog and books, Bernadette had built a bond with her readers and wanted to form a deeper connection with them. And through my adventures in the world of baking and bakeries, I knew first hand how the connections we make with our customers and our community can pull us along through life's challenges.

We thought it would feel good to get to know these folks better and we suspected that they would enjoy getting to know each other too. And if they connected with each other more deeply, our members would find what they needed to build businesses and ship projects that matched their values and purpose.

That was it. That was the whole plan. And wow, has it ever worked! Almost immediately, the Right Company shifted away from Bernadette and her readers. It became all about connection between members; sharing ideas, supporting each other and building things together. This book is their biggest collaboration so far and I am thrilled to see it released into the world.

There was one big mistake in our original plan, however. I thought that we were each missing something which prevented us from getting what we wanted from life. A blind spot, a missing skill or a key bit of knowledge. I thought that the group would help individual members fill in their gaps.

But that's not the case. What I have learned is that each of these beautiful people is fully formed. They each have exactly what they need to live a life of creativity and purpose. To build businesses that serve them along with their employees and their customers. That is, they are already enough.

This collection of essays, poems and stories span a myriad of professions, locations and life experiences, but they each reflect the deep care and purpose of their author. Wonderful humans who I am honoured to call my friends.

These stories can be a mirror into your life as well. As you read on, I am confident that you will find a passage or an image that connects with you and your experiences. A reminder that you are enough, just as you are.

About Jeremy Deedes

Jeremy Deedes is a life coach and founder of Crazy for Change, a programme for the overwhelmed and frustrated which coaches people to live meaningfully by helping others to find meaning in their lives.

After many ups and downs, Jeremy finds himself in a good place and provides the programme so that others can benefit from his mistakes made and lessons learnt. He helps clients develop the life skills needed to overcome today's tremendous social and economic challenges and free themselves to find happiness, grow their resilience and wealth, and make a difference.

He pursued his passion for coaching after selling his financial life planning business in 2016. He also volunteers as a trustee for an education and career development charity. He holds an MBA, a Postgraduate Certificate in Coaching and is enrolled on a master's degree in psychology.

Jeremy is the author of the acclaimed book *Right Money, Right Place, Right Time*, in which he sets out a methodology for wholehearted, meaningful living. Jeremy has also contributed to *Retire Inspire*, an anthology of essays on making the most of retirement. He lives in Yorkshire in the UK and is married with one son. A Madagascan Ratting Dog (who has never caught a rat in her life) and two black cats share the family home. Jeremy counts cycling, walking, and reading amongst his interests.

Meet Jeremy at:
https://wordsnotdeeds.co.uk
https://crazyforchange.com
https://www.linkedin.com/in/jeremydeedescoach/

On the Threshold:
An Introduction to Enough

Jeremy Deedes (UK)

The global collective pause of 2020/21 precipitated fundamental questions in the minds of many of us about our future lives and work. Whilst money remains a strong motivator, care of and connection with self, family, friends, and the wider community is becoming a more critical part of our agendas. We are no longer asking, how much is enough? Instead, we are asking, what is enough? Research supports this.

- A WHO/ILO report suggests that long hours are killing hundreds of thousands [1]. The statistics show that, in 2018, a working week over 55 hours increased the chance of death by stroke or heart disease significantly. Pressure for change is already intense, and governments, employers, and workers are considering limiting working hours through legislation, flexible working, and job sharing. Many will be inclined to accept that a potentially lower income is a price worth paying for a better lifestyle.

- According to a recent NatWest/YouGov survey, five per cent (one in 20) of all under-35s in the UK started their own business in 2020 [2]. However, this figure rose to 15 per cent (one in seven) for those starting or considering their own business in 2021. The indications are that workers are switching off from organisations that rule their lives. They no longer wish to be shoehorned into a workspace that is not theirs. Their strategy for a better life seems to be to regain control by becoming their own boss.

- The UK's Office of National Statistics in 2020 found that nearly 30% of 16 to 69-year-olds are planning on making significant changes to their lives, especially in their work, relationships and home arenas[3]. These people seem to recognise the scarcity in their lives, whether of money, company, control or fun. However, although they may have intentions, they may not know how to make a move.

It seems many of us are contemplating a complete head re-set as aspirations and priorities are redrawn. We want to know if there is a different and better way of doing things. We are asking if we can adapt, innovate and change without losing our skills and experience, and if so, how. But, above all, we are asking about what is enough in terms of time, money, happiness, success, friendships etc.

Thinking about enough

This book is an anthology of stories written by the Right Company (tRC) members that seek to address these questions and concerns. The Right Company is an online global gathering of professionals and entrepreneurs founded in 2018 by Bernadette Jiwa in Australia and Mark Dyck in Canada. It is a forum for providing support, sharing achievements and exchanging ideas around our businesses. However, members of tRC are driven as much by their values, vision, goals, ambitions, and community responsibilities as they are by money. Therefore, it is not surprising that our online chats and calls often gravitate to what is enough and how we can manage our businesses to deliver enough of all that we need.

This book emerged from one of those discussions, galvanising us to use our stories to encourage, inspire, and widen horizons. We are not celebrities or members of the glitterati. We are ordinary people who have experienced the ups and downs of life and work. We have made mistakes, learnt lessons, and oscillatcd between abundance and scarcity. This book is an anthology of the stories, lessons, and achievements we hope will provide you with comfort and motivation as well as the incentive to rethink your definition of enough.

Of course, we don't know who you are. However, you will probably be in business or a profession, although you may work in the charitable sector or government / NGOs. Crucially, you will be dissatisfied, even fed up, with your work and life, and you are interested in finding out how you can earn enough money whilst following your heart. You will probably hate the thought of working all your life for someone else, only to be retired at 60 or 65. You don't want a work hangover but want to keep contributing until it becomes physically impossible.

Defining enough is crucial for you, as is how to achieve it and overcome the fear, failures, and other challenges that significant change often precipitates. And whilst the after-effects of the Pandemic are a powerful catalyst for change, you are more likely to want to be defined by your path, achievements and individuality than the Pandemic.

Tap into our stories

The authors of this book have been in your shoes. We have heartfelt and often moving stories to tell of our achievements and failures, stories that can inspire, encourage and open up your mind to the abundance of possibilities available in the world.

Most tRC members have long shunned those who wanted to tell us what to do and found new furrows to plough. We have evolved from the corporate world into the entrepreneurial world (and sometimes back again). We will keep on doing so. We are free agents with no plans to retire but to keep evolving and contributing.

We are a geographically, culturally and linguistically diverse group of people sharing a common interest in doing right by ourselves, our families and communities without being shackled by the rules and structures of larger organisations. We have many different views on what enough means for us, why we do what we do and how we got there.

We describe what we have done successfully to occupy the liminal space between our personal and professional lives. This space lacks the precise definition and boundaries found in more structured occupations. We describe what enough looks like for us in financial and life terms and tell how we defined our goals and values and got to where we are now. Many of us write about how we see our journey as more important than the destination with no ultimate end in mind and how we have gotten away from living someone else's definition of success.

We write about how we have used our time, our most precious commodity, to best effect and how we have re-structured our days and hours to make more time for things other than earning money. Achieving temporal freedom is a goal more important than money, to which many will aspire.

We can offer techniques and practices for achieving that freedom, and so you will find commentaries here about both why we have chosen our paths and how we have done it.

Many of the accounts in this book are intense and often profoundly moving. Therefore, we have included shorter pieces between the chapters that we hope offer a more light-hearted view of our lives and work. You will find quirky stories, favourite quotes, memes and other ephemera that illustrate our lives that were and our lives that we live today.

The promise and challenge of this book

The book promises that you, who aspire to live a fulfilled and wholehearted life with enough money, discretionary time and integrity, will get thought-provoking advice, guidance and inspiration derived from the diverse experiences and lessons of tRC.

We hope our contributions to this book will be mind-expanding, inspirational and motivational. But, above all, we hope you will enjoy them and take heart from them.

References

[1] Pega, F et al. (2021). Global, regional, and national burdens of ischemic heart disease and stroke attributable to exposure to long working hours for 194 countries, 2000–2016: A systematic analysis from the WHO/ILO Joint Estimates of the Work-related Burden of Disease and Injury. Environment International, vol 154, accessed from https://www.sciencedirect.com/science/article/pii/S0160412021002208on 19 July 2021

[2] https://www.telegraph.co.uk/news/2021/05/16/britains-yolo-generation-three-times-many-millennials-planning/

[3] Office for National Statistics (2020).Coronavirus and the social impacts on Great Britain. Accessed from https://www.ons.gov.uk/peoplepopulationandcommunity/healthandsocialcare/healthandwellbeing/bulletins/coronavirusandthesocialimpactsongreatbritain/26june2020on 19 July 2021. This regular survey contained an additional section (§6) asking respondents about their long term intentions.

The Breaths We Take

Jeremy Deedes (UK)

My friend was an amateur jockey who died aged just 37 after a fall in a race in 2021. I had known her almost since her birth and watched her grow up on her parents' farm on the Hereford Wales border.

Horses were her life. They were her passion and her reason for getting up in the morning, for living a life that was meaningful and fulfilled.

My friend loved winning but accepted defeat with grace and good humour. She was both free-spirited and adventurous as well as generous with her time and friendship.

She had worked out what was enough, and encapsulated it by hanging this well-known quote on the wall of the stables:

Life is not measured by the number of breaths we take, but by the moments that take our breath away.

She took far fewer breaths and probably experienced many more breath-taking moments than most of us. She had worked out what gave her life meaning and what was enough.

About Kim LeClair

Kim LeClair is a freelance web designer based in Wheaton, IL. She started her practice, East Willow, in 2012. Never one for the traditional path, she earned a master's degree in Cognitive Psychology and then began a winding career thru the non-profit and government sectors doing both program development and training. Her last job was at a large healthcare organization as a manager in the IT department. Early in 2012, she took the jump out of corporate and into the great wide open and she hasn't looked back since. Well, maybe she has a little.

Since then, she has been creating websites for aspiring freelancers and entrepreneurs, helping them build an online presence that fits who they are and what they want to contribute to the world.

Kim enjoys performing long form improv and in 2020 started a daily practice of writing one poem a day. No promises the poems are any good, but she writes them nonetheless.

Meet Kim at:
https://eastwillow.com

Great Quests Don't Come with Maps

Kim LeClair (USA)

Touchstones in the quest to build a life that fits who we are and what we have to offer the world

Think about heroes you know, characters like Luke Sky-walker, Bilbo and Frodo Baggins, and Hermione Granger. They each experienced epic adventures but when they started, they had no idea where they were going or what to expect. They didn't have a map. They learned as they went along, both about the world and about themselves.

We are all on an adventure of sorts. I would even call it a quest. A quest to build a work life and a life that fits who we are and what we have to offer the world. But ... where to start? How to orient? What matters? How do we define success?

I am going to take you on a little metaphorical journey for the next few hundred words. A journey informed by the last ten years of my own life, as I have built a small freelance web design business. I have discovered three touchstones along the way that I would like to share with you:

- Clarity
- Confidence
- Consistency

I hope that sharing them along with some of my own story will help you on your own journey. Are you ready to begin? Adventure awaits!

....

Imagine a road stretched out in front of us. Along the road in the distance you see three waypoints, small shelters where you can take a short break and reflect on where you are and where you are going.

This beginning, this staring down the road and not quite knowing what is ahead, is how I began my own freelance journey. I imagined myself earning money building websites for people but that was the extent of my plan. When I look back now, I marvel at my bravado, or perhaps it was recklessness! I guess all great quests start with a little bit of bravery. We've come to the first waypoint, a covered shelter. Inside we see a book on the wooden bench … It is titled "*What do you want? What do they want?*" This is where we find our first touchstone of **Clarity**.

Some of the questions we encounter here include:

- Do you know what you want your business and life to be?
- Are you being as clear as possible with others about what you can offer them?

Could someone else describe what you do?

- Why are you doing this?
- Who are you doing it for?
- What is your process?
- What will you charge?

These questions are important to answer. Yet, in the beginning, you may only have the slightest sketch of your replies. Looking back on my experiences, I see that I developed clarity organically by trying things and then reflecting on the experience. These reflections took two forms – looking inward and looking outward:

- Inward. Did I enjoy this? Do I want to do more of it? Does this feel like my unique work?
- Outward. Do people seem to want or need this? Do they understand it when I share my offering with them?

When I quit my job ten years ago, I longed to do something more creative. Now, with years of freelancing experience behind me, I see that my deeper longing was for autonomy. I understand now that my optimal way of working allows me to follow my own inspirational urges, to craft my own schedule, and also to be directly of service.

Over the past ten years I have also increased my outward clarity about my customers. I know more about who my ideal customers are and I understand them more clearly. I have more empathy for my clients' struggles and their own deeper longings. I can speak more clearly about what I do and who I do it for.

Allow yourself to consider your own clarity. Remember, gaining inward and outward clarity will unfold over time and space. You won't know everything right away. That's ok. Remember, it's an adventure! For now, let's keep on going, shall we?

....

Now we arrive at the second waypoint with a wooden bench and another book, open to a page with the following question in big bold letters — *"Are you SURE you can do this??"* Here we have reached the touchstone of **Confidence**.

Confidence is defined as the belief or certainty that things will turn out, that we are up for the challenge. And we also all know that in the dark of night confidence can disappear like a drop of water on a hot skillet. Fear lurks in the back of all of our minds.

Confidence, like clarity, has two sides – internal and external. Internal confidence is your own sense of being able to accomplish something, do your work well. External confidence relates to how much others trust you.

It is a common thing for a friend or caring loved one to say, "*you can do it!*" but my experience is that it is only in my doing a thing that I begin to trust and believe. It is through action that I find my internal confidence. For me, confidence is like a muscle. I have to use it and strengthen it by doing my work, my reps, in the world. There is no substitute.

In my own work, I have seen my confidence grow exponentially. For instance, I used to worry that on an initial call with a new client I might not know the answers to their questions or would somehow mess up my chances of working with them. Now, after hundreds of these calls, I don't worry that I won't have the answers. I have confidence in my own skills and knowledge. If I don't have an answer for some reason, I am comfortable enough to say that. This is the kind of internal confidence that grew for me over time. It came through doing the work.

External confidence is bound up in your reputation. When someone refers a friend to you, they demonstrate trust. When a previous client contacts you about a question, or returns for more business, they are showing they have confidence in you. Testimonials are a display of trust and confidence in your work. External confidence could just as easily be called trust.

Simply put: Do your potential customers trust you? Do they think you are the right person for the job?

Just as internal confidence is a bit like a muscle that takes time to build, trust develops over time. You have to be in the marketplace, demonstrating your competence. Trust will grow as you follow through, treat people with respect and dignity, value your customers, honestly serve them, keep your promises. This has been my experience.

I have been so very lucky to build my business slowly, over time, all through trusted referrals. I know this isn't possible for all of us, but no matter your type of service or product, trust will be a factor in the purchasing decisions of your potential customers. Keep this touchstone close, it really matters. Take it seriously. Strengthen the muscle.

....

We don't have unlimited time, so we need to keep on going. Here we stop at our third and final waypoint, and upon this wooden bench are stacks and stacks of paper all with the same word written on them ... that word is again ... again ... again ... again ... This is the touchstone of **Consistency**.

Consistency is the drum beat, the march ever forward. It is showing up as a web designer even when you don't have a project. It is following up to say thank you when someone refers to you. It is delivering on time. Consistency is all the work that you do over and over again that demonstrates to both you and to others that this work is for real. Consistency demonstrates your professionalism.

For me to create consistency in my work I need:

- A schedule that is flexible but structured
- A workspace that is dedicated to work
- To stay connected with people

- To get adequate sleep
- To move my body on a regular basis

If these things drop away, I see that I get less efficient, less consistent. When that happens I have to bring them back into my life, over and over and over again. Sticking with something for the long haul makes a huge difference. The truth is that simply hanging on, showing up day after day, matters.

Consistency can also look like staying with the work you are clear about and not being pulled off center by distractions. Consistency can mean saying no more often than you might be used to. This kind of consistency continues to be a challenge for me. Even 10 years in, I still have a tendency to want to just respond to whatever the moment is bringing. But I have also found that by building routines and schedules (that work for me) I am better at my work and also just better overall.

Look at your favorite brand. When you see that brand show up using the same colors and general visual look over different marketing channels, this is consistency at work. It creates recognizability and that matters. Using the same words, the same tagline consistently over time creates awareness and trust. And it creates a story, both in our own minds and in the minds of our customers. It creates the space in the world that was not there before, the space in which we do our work.

Do you keep your promises? Do you show up and deliver, leading people to trust you? Keep doing that, over and over, consistently. That is what this touchstone is all about.

....

We are reaching the end of our metaphorical journey together. Up ahead we see the marketplace. A bustling square of people and ideas. As you enter, the touchstones you have collected, **Clarity**, **Confidence**, and **Consistency**, will lead you forward. Remember these are yours to hold and develop. They are not determined by others but by you. How you craft your work life and your life life is up to you. This is a great privilege.

As you walk this journey and learn along the way, you become a modern hero. Your adventure leads you to the place all heroes find, your place of **Contribution**.

Great quests don't come with maps, but I hope these concepts of Clarity, Confidence, and Consistency help you to draw your own.

We are in the marketplace waiting for your **Contribution**.

About Sue Heatherington

Sue Heatherington offers fresh sight from the quiet edge and believes that our words shape our reality. She is an established writer and professional thinking partner from a little valley in South West Wales with a background in senior executive leadership and pioneering change.

Sue coined the phrase quiet disruptor as a founding member of *the Right Company* in 2018, and her book *Quiet Disruptors: Creating Change Without Shouting* has been read across the globe.

Her short daily blogs combine words of inspiration, provocation and encouragement, with a beautiful photograph from her home in the valley, which she shares with her husband, learning disabled brother and a herd of alpacas.

Meet Sue at:
https://thewaterside.co.uk/
https://quietdisruptors.com/
linkedin.com/in/sue-heatherington-98a87013
https://twitter.com/SueWaterside

There are Days

Sue Heatherington (UK)

Sometimes
there are days
when only
part of us
seems in focus.
That is enough.

About Jacquie Landeman

Jacquie Landeman doesn't have a job title but she does have a much-loved j.o.b. in a small finance company in Auckland, New Zealand, working for a team that inspires and encourages innovation and out-of-the-box thinking. Her passion lies in the customer experience which she does with a heart full of care and a passion for serving. When she's not working, she volunteers as a budgeting coach for Christians Against Poverty, runs a women's group, organises street parties, is a member of *the Right Company*, occasionally blogs, and more recently has been facing her fear of public speaking at Toastmasters.

Meet Jacquie at:
https://www.linkedin.com/in/jacquie-l-26199038/
https://distillations.blog/

Enough with the Rules

Jacquie Landeman (New Zealand)

*One of the most effective ways of finding meaning
and purpose in your work is to start with kindness.*

Rules and procedures provide us with guardrails on how to handle certain situations within our organizations. They often come about due to a negative experience that is upsetting enough that a decision is made to document it, as a way of preventing a recurrence.

In theory, this seems like a good practice except that rules brought about by a negative experience tend to tar all customers with the same brush. When we use our policies, procedures, and rule books as the definitive guide for how we do business we mostly spend our time defending and justifying those policies to customers who want and deserve more.

The rule book can seem helpful when it comes to making customer-service decisions – a quick yes or no. Box ticked. Job done. The one-size-fits-all rule book may make following procedures easier but what happens to the customer experience?

Here is the question I like to ask myself: "*What would be helpful here?*" rather than "*What is the rule/policy/procedure here?*"

If you've ever spent time justifying to a customer why you can't or won't do what he is requesting you know how time-consuming that can be. The more you resist him, the more he leans in. You end up feeling frustrated because, in your eyes, you're doing your job, adhering to the rules and following procedure yet your customer is vocalising in all the ways he can, that "*you don't care about ME at all*"!

And he means that literally. He doesn't care about the collective procedure and policies that form your business and cover all customers. He cares only about the experience he is having with you and the problem he needs to be solved.

I work as a lender in the finance sector where there are rules, procedures, and regulations, a-plenty.

When a customer contacts us for more lending and her account is in arrears, the answer according to the rule book is *"your loan must be current before we can top up your account"*. This answer creates a new problem for our customer. She doesn't have the means to pay for the arrears and her need for a top-up is real.

This was the case for Marlene, a customer since 2012 who missed two payments a month ago. I had a choice that day. Stick to the rule book and do my job or ask what would be helpful? The solution was easy … Reset her account so it's current. Show her grace as a long-term, valued customer. Help quickly without her having to plead her case. Let her get on with what she needs to do today without getting in her way. Let it be something today that went easily.

What if we were kinder than necessary, kinder than expected?[1] What if we keep believing the best about people, even when we've had the odd experience that's left us feeling bruised? What if instead of closing a door or making a rule or adding a hoop, we keep working on ways to give more, not less? What if we made helping, our first operational policy? Not as something that comes up later, when we are trying to patch up a relationship that's gone astray?

It comes down to grace and empathy – putting yourself in your customer's shoes and imagining for a moment what it might be like if you were going through the same thing.

I heard a story on a podcast about empathy recently, where the host, John, spoke about a negative experience he had with a car rental company where they had charged him a late fee when in fact he had returned the car early. Instead of believing him, the customer service rep told John he would have to write to their head office to have the matter reviewed. So, John redirected his frustration to Twitter. Suddenly the company responded with a no-questions-asked refund. John remarked that while he appreciated the refund, he would never, ever use that company again.

The thing is so many companies work like this. They operate from the rule book and then move into damage control when they come up against opposition that threatens their image. Shouldn't we be considering our image from the outset – as an opportunity to enhance our customer's experience and build a relationship?

By the way, a sure sign that a company is letting rules and policy dictate how their customers are treated is when you see posters that say, "*please don't be rude to our staff.*" Anytime I see that kind of signage at a customer service counter, I brace myself for … less.

Customers don't come in looking to fight – they come in to solve a problem. When they get upset it's normally because we have added some element of stress to their day via our resistance. If signs have to be erected to ask customers not to yell at your staff, it's probably time to ask, "*why are they yelling*"?

Let's use our rules and policies as a guide but held lightly.

When a customer pushes back or demands more, let's treat the interaction as a valuable source of honest feedback. Put down the rule book, stop defending it and listen. Find out why she is upset? What would make for a better experience? How are our policies or rules getting in the way of where she wants to be?

A few years back I did Bernadette Jiwa's, Story Strategy course. (https://thestorystrategy.com) This course was instrumental in helping me gain understanding and insights into what it was like to walk in our customer's shoes. Getting clear on our customer's worldview, became a springboard for new and innovative ways to be more … helpful … because now we were thinking from her perspective – not ours. For me, it was also the turning point for finding meaning and joy in my work. In finance!

There are opportunities every day for me to stand on policy, procedure, and regulations. But I stopped doing that because it was incredibly draining. Justifying and defending rules and policies takes way more time and energy than simply choosing to be helpful from the get-go.

Plus helping, really helping, means I get to the end of my day and I don't have a work hangover. The kind that a day spent resisting used to give me – where I would cycle between feeling less-than-good about myself while also justifying my way of being, on the rule book, I followed.

It can be exhausting defending a policy – much better to push it aside and to ask … "*what would be helpful here? How can I show unexpected kindness?*" And when I say that I mean not with conditions, like "*I'll do this for you this time, but next time you had better …* "

Instead, make your response something like, *"yes of course I can help, let me do that for you now."* We don't need to make them feel wrong because they missed a payment. To paraphrase Jesus (John 8:7), *"Please throw the first stone you who haven't ....* *[missed a payment or forgot to / couldn't meet a commitment] before"*.

In his book **The Speed of Trust**, Steven M. R. Covey says that *"Trust always affects two outcomes: speed and cost. When trust goes down, speed goes down and cost goes up. When trust goes up, speed goes up and cost goes down"*.

He uses 9/11 as an example. Before 9/11 – he would arrive at his local airport 30 minutes before a flight. Now he needs to be there 2-3 hours ahead of departure to allow time for all the security procedures. And of course, the cost of travel increased due to additional taxes.

For me, deciding to let a customer top up their account when they have arrears, as in Marlene's case, is proof that Steven M. R. Covey's formula works. Time and cost-saving for both of us. The path ahead made clear to move forward, without friction or fight. The relationship strengthened. Trust, a gift for both of us.

Part of my work is in credit control, and the same principles work there. Instead of following the credit-control manual of demands and threats, we start with how can we help? Not being able to meet a payment is hard and often people feel scared to talk about their situation, particularly if they have been treated unkindly by other creditors.

When someone's missing payments, she's not trying to rip off the system. She's not a crook. She is someone who just needs to be able to talk about what's going on without judgment. She needs understanding. From that place, rules aside – let grace do its magic. Grace says, "*It's ok, don't worry. Let's see what we can do to help.*"

I have this quote stuck to my computer. It reminds me that the change I seek to make starts and ends with caring about the people I serve.

....

"*You might not be able to change how the world values your profession but you can change how you are valued by doing work that matters. Work that changes how people feel, not just what they think.*" Bernadette Jiwa

....

So ENOUGH –

- With the rules and the policies and the regulations at least in terms of how they shape your work.
- Enough with holding the weight of resistance.
- Enough with justification and defensiveness.

Drop the rule book, down tool the procedures, and see what happens when kindness, grace, and trust lead your work.

References

[1] This is Principle 6 from the 10 Guiding Principles For Co-Creating A Positive Future, the collaborative work of members from *the Right Company* created in mid-2020 to re-imagine our work life after Covid. https://future-manifesto.com

....

Enough of Me

Jacqueline Davis (USA)

I've seen how people treat other plants.
How they fawn and fuss and pray over them.
They give them the best fertilizer and water, and just the right amount of sunshine.
They grow to be big, beautiful plants.
And they're so upset if something happens to one.
As if Mother Nature is against them.

They enter them into flower shows and then run around smiling at judges, hoping to get their hands on a ribbon – 1st place, 2nd place, 3rd place, honorable mention.
But they don't mention me.
It's as though I'm a terrible word. Huh!
I don't need any special light or food or water. I am strong. I am a survivor.
I can grow in the harshest of conditions. All kinds of environments.
You may see me peeking out from between cracks in the sidewalk.
Sometimes I push through crevices in walls.
Or, grow alongside highways in the brush next to foul-smelling water.

Cars ride over me.
Feet trample me.
And you can't imagine what dogs do to me. Or, can you?
And they gasp at how unsightly I am.
Unsightly? They want me to believe that I'm unsightly. But that's not what I see.
I see long, beautiful green stems that curve and twist and turn and bend.
Sometimes with vibrant yellow flowers or fluffy tops that blow in the wind.
I show the prettiest purple flowers. It all depends on how I feel.
And, I feel gorgeous. I am gorgeous!
No one looks after me. I look after myself. I'm a survivor.
At some point, I was intro-duced deliberately. People said I was beneficial. But when I began to proliferate, they said I was invasive. A nuisance.

They pull me out when they've had enough of me and want to beautify the environment.
But I grow back...stronger. My roots are deep.
Sometimes they spray me with poisonous chemicals only to find out years later that they have poisoned themselves.
I'm called many names – goldenrod, dandelion, ama-ranth, and ragweed.
Yes, I am a weed. A strong, beautiful weed.
And, a weed by any other name is still a survivor.
Might I be an inspiration to you?

About Caroline Harvey

Caroline is a public speaking coach and facilitator. Growing up in Wales, the Land of Song, shaped her belief in the power of language and voice to enchant our audience.

She has lived and worked in diverse countries, from Europe to Japan and back. And hopped around in the corporate communications world, crossing cultural and language barriers. Pulling together threads, and weaving them into stories.

A sometime poet, occasional clown and Jane Austen fan, Caroline is on a mission to help people cut through the noise without shouting. To move their audience by being themselves – leveraging their singular voice and the creative power of words.

She coaches leaders, executives and entrepreneurs to speak with natural presence and confidently shape change. And she designs and delivers bespoke workshops for clients, building on her business experience and integrating performing arts techniques to spark creativity.

Caroline lives south of Barcelona, right where the mountains meet the sea. Her two children having flown the nest, she lives with her husband and a brown shaggy dog called Phoebe.

Meet Caroline at:
https://www.carolineharveyimpact.com/
https://www.linkedin.com/in/caroharvey/
www.carolineharvey.me

It all Started with a Red Nose

Caroline Harvey (Spain)

My story of a quest to reconnect with myself,
rediscover my creativity ... and face down my fears.

The first time I stepped onto a stage, alone, I was wearing a red nose. It was the first session of a clown workshop I'd signed up for, and I had to follow one simple instruction: Just be, and see what happens. I remember all too clearly what happened. My heart was pounding, my stomach in knots. Like a rabbit in the headlights I felt exposed, vulnerable ... and terrified. I couldn't even look at my friendly audience of would-be clowns. I cast my eyes around frantically for somewhere to hide – nowhere – so I walked over to the window and stared fixedly out onto the corrugated roof below, as if it were fascinating. And I willed it to be over. Quiet and introverted, I'd shied away from the spotlight all my life. I readily helped others to shine, but would run in the other direction if asked to speak in public.

The clown workshop made a bold promise: to help rediscover the pleasure of play, our sense of humour and ability to laugh at ourselves. Clowning is about connecting with the inner child, that playful spirit we all have but tend to lose sight of as we get older, conditioned as we are to do, achieve and comply.

"We don't become adults, we become adulterated," [1] as Tortell Poltrona, founder of **Payasos Sin Fronteras** (Clowns Without Borders) put it. Our clowns live in the moment, and don't bow to convention.

After that inauspicious start I began to trust in my teacher [2], my clowning classmates and myself, and something magical took place. Putting on the red nose opened a portal to my inner clown, and she started to make her appearance. Timidly at first. And then she roared into life.

Through those workshops, I discovered that my clown is expressive. And creative. And makes people laugh. This was the first milestone on the quest to find my voice. Sometime later I joined a theatre group, then a public speaking club. When I stepped in front of an audience, something had shifted. I was still nervous for sure … but I also felt the stirrings of empowerment.

I decided to apply this discovery to my work. After a career in corporate communications, I had set up a business helping companies shape their messages for international audiences. I was working with leaders and executives to help them make better presentations, and to feel better about making them.

I knew first-hand that standing in front of an audience can have us quaking in our boots. And that this is written in our DNA: being alone and exposed in front of many pairs of eyes flips us into the fight, flight or freeze response. It was that ancient reflex that led me to escape out the window in clown class, before letting the red nose work its magic. As my quest continued I found other alternatives to hide behind: a character in a play. Or a well-rehearsed speech with a carefully crafted script. But what if I took away those props? Appeared without the red nose? What if I removed the veneer of performance and stood there, as myself?

In her book **Presence: Bringing Your Boldest Self To Your Biggest Challenges**, Harvard Business School professor Amy Cuddy claims,"… *the more we are able to be ourselves, the more we are able to be present. And that makes us convincing.*"[3]

I knew the key to helping my clients was to show them how to take off the professional mask and bring their whole selves to their business presentations. To be truly present. I had seen and felt the wondrous effect when that happened. There was energy, connection and engagement. But I still didn't quite know what that meant for me.

To practice what I preached with passion and integrity I had to continue the search for my voice. Not the voice that sought approval and changed timbre to please others. Or that fitted in and followed convention. But my true voice – however that may sound. This became a quest to reconnect with myself, rediscover my creativity … and face down my fears.

Remember that reflex of reaching for props to feel safe and secure? My approach to life meant that I researched and re-hearsed, checked and controlled … held on to all the guy ropes just in case a gust of wind blew the tent away. It was like a never-ending game of Twister. Except this game wasn't fun. It was exhausting, and unsustainable.

To continue on my quest for self-realisation, I had to let go of those ropes. So I did. And against all expectations, the tent didn't blow away. Not only was it still standing, but it had billowed out to become much larger, to let in air and light and life. By releasing the tension I had created space, and opportunity. I began to expand to fill that space. To rekindle my creativity. And embrace my personal story.

Growing up in Wales – the Land of Song – had shaped my love of language and belief in the power of voice. This was something I had always felt, but now it was time to share it properly. With empathy, and generosity.

Here's the thing: whatever line of work we are in, we are all communicators. I wholly understand what my clients go through when they compare making a presentation to diving into an empty swimming pool. I have been there. But I also know they have the resources – professional and personal – to overcome those fears, and make a difference. It is so tempting to look for an escape rather than into the eyes of our audience. To hide behind our knowledge and expertise, and many, many slides.

The central tenets of my client work are, in fact, what I discovered on my quest. In an interview with Robert Macfarlane, a Fellow at the University of Cambridge and author of the book **Underland: A Deep Time Journey**, Krista Tippett refers to Macfarlane's interpretation of the word discover – "*to reveal by excavation: fetch up from the depths*"[4]. Excavating takes effort. But it is worth it. My learnings shape not only my approach to speaking in public, but to my business, and life in general.

1. Less is more

We don't need to say that much to share meaning. The busier our content, the less people will hear. We can distil our business narrative down to its purest essence – derived in no small part from the presence of the person sharing it.

According to Amy Cuddy, "*Presence stems from believing and trusting your story – your feelings, beliefs, values and abilities…. Presence isn't about pretending to be competent; it's about believing in and revealing the abilities you truly have. It's about shedding whatever is blocking you from expressing who you are.*"[5] As well as concise content, audiences want to see the person behind it.

2. Ma

One of the most powerful techniques for moving our audience is by saying ... nothing. The Japanese word Ma illustrates this perfectly. Ma refers to a pause or interval, the time and space that allows for growth, and creativity.

"Ma is filled with nothing but energy and feeling. It speaks of silence as opposed to sound, of lack as opposed to excess. It is the momentary pause in speech needed to convey meaningful words, the silence between the notes that make the music ... There is a need for Ma in every aspect and every day of our lives."[6]

The Japanese kanji symbol for Ma combines the characters for door, and sun. Together they depict a door opened just enough to let sunlight in.[7]

Pauses are the chinks of light that illuminate what we have to say. Before we start speaking. To highlight our message. And to herald the close. Our role is to take our audience on a journey. As their guide, we need to trust in ourselves. Release the guy ropes and give our audience – and ourselves – space to breathe. Ma is an absence – but one that speaks volumes.

3. A sense of play

Our subject matter may be serious, but the most effective way to spark imagination and curiosity is by being playful. Telling a story, or using images – literal and figurative. Connecting playfully with our sense of self gives us access to our unique treasure trove of stories, cultural references, and imagery: jewels that light up our communications. And make people smile.

To connect with our audience and be truly present, we don't need to attract attention with bells, whistles, or slides. And we don't need to wear a red nose to feel our clown with energy, presence and space. We simply need to be ourselves. In the moment.

Rather than making or doing a presentation, we are our presentation. In business – as in life – we can give ourselves permission to take off the mask and communicate as people. Speaking not just from the head, but from the heart. Sharing our gift of knowledge, or perspective. With vulnerability, authenticity, and humanity.

The truth is, I am enough. And so are you.

[1] Interview with Tortell Poltrona in diarioimagen.net, https://www.diarioimagen.net/?p=459247 - 10 February 2020

[2] Dominique Hudson, soul therapist, working with Theatre, Improvisation and Clown.

[3] Amy Cuddy – Presence: Bringing Your Boldest Self To Your Biggest Challenges, page 29 (Kindle version), Little, Brown & Company, 2015

[4] Robert Macfarlane was a guest on 'The Worlds Beneath Our Feet', Episode 962 of the podcast On Being, with Krista Tippett (3 June 2021)

[5] Amy Cuddy - Presence: Bringing Your Boldest Self To Your Biggest Challenges, page 28 (Kindle version), Little, Brown & Company, 2015

[6] https://new.uniquejapan.com/ikebana/ma/

[7] https://new.uniquejapan.com/ikebana/ma/

We are not lost ...

Sue Heatherington (UK)

We are not lost ...
we just need to pause,
put away our
old maps,
see where we are
with fresh eyes,
hear the sound
of the world
with open ears,
and make
a new path.
Together.

About Pete Michaels

Pete Michaels works with entrepreneurs and growing businesses to help them better communicate their unique value to the right people.

He helps independent service providers like coaches and consultants, startups and SMBs better understand their best clients and customers in order to create messaging that resonates more deeply with them. Pete calls this blend of branding and direct response copywriting Selling Unique.

Meet Pete at:
https://rockandrollcopy.com
linkedin.com/in/peter-michaels-a4204348

A Question of Perspective

Pete Michaels (UK / Germany)

*How I decided to stop trying to live up to the expectations of
others, and start doing business on my own terms.*

There are many reasons for starting a business – some intentional, others less so. Over the years of running my own solo business and working with other biz-owners, I've come to accept that some very good ideas, happy lives and successful ventures actually grew out of someone starting something without really knowing what the hell they were doing. Which is great. I was one of them.

It also turns out that many people find themselves doing a particular type of work – often very successfully – as a consequence of having rejected all the other options at some point. That may sound like a bit of a negative approach, but it's a valid way to begin a career outside of a regular J.O.B. It's pretty much how I started mine.

The thing about beginnings is: they don't have to be carried around forever like heavy baggage. They're to be done, moved on from and left behind. Even the beginnings of things end up as the past.

For many people – like me, and probably you since you're reading this book – the idea of being employed, having a boss and serving a purpose defined by someone or something else has a very limited appeal. And that appeal tends to run out around the time we realise we're unhappy with that option and are staring at another ten, twenty or forty years of the same thing before being able to cash in on that company pension and retire to do … the things we would rather be doing now.

So we throw in the towel, kick over the franking machine, punch the boss in the face and clock off for the final time, striding elatedly towards the promised land of self-employment. We decide it's time to do our own thing, to start a business and give ourselves the freedom to create, connect and trade under our own name. But what if we don't yet know exactly what it is we're about to do? Who to serve? What to create? It's too late to turn back (the franking machine has been replaced but the old boss isn't exactly in forgiving mood) so we'd better get on with it. Because the truth is, some of us just aren't cut out for Having A Job.

This can be a challenging concept for the newly-self-employed or recently-fired to share with spouses, parents, friends, accountants and jaded authority figures who just need to know exactly how we intend to pay what we owe Organisation X with dreams and ideas. But the World Of Work doesn't need to be all work and no play (although there is some work involved, otherwise it would just be called the World Of Play).

Thankfully, it is possible to build a business with yourself at the centre, to find fulfilment in your work, to do your own thing and feel like you're making a valuable contribution in your own unique way. Enough people have shown that this can be done – even if we know, deep down, that the Hollywood biopics and household names are the exceptions rather than the rule. You don't have to be set on reinventing the wheel or changing the orbit of the moon, or buying an island five years after landing your first client. There are other treasures to reach for, other parts of the journey to enjoy.

So, what if you don't want to be the next Elon Musk or Oprah Winfrey or Richard Branson – you just want to do something you'll enjoy, work with good people, get paid well for it and have some laughs along the way? Even those reasonable-sounding ambitions can seem a long way off when you're starting out. But take heart, because you have something nobody else has, or ever had before. (Elon, Oprah and Sir Rick certainly don't have it. They can't even buy it.)

You have YOU. Your hits and misses, your hard-learned lessons, your ways of moving on from one high or low point to another: nobody else has ever done things in quite the same way before. Over the years it's taken you to reach this point right here, right now, you have amassed a completely unique combination of skills, personality and experience. That unique combination has untold value. It will help you attract clients, customers and collaborators. It will give you strength on those occasions when you doubt yourself or what you have to offer (this WILL happen, it's part of the process).

In my own work as a copywriter (sort of – we'll come back to definitions in a minute) and salesperson-in-print for growing entrepreneurial businesses, I focus on helping my clients understand and express their unique value, their one-in-a-zillion combinations. I call it Selling Unique – the idea that what makes you YOU is a key part of your product or services' appeal to others.

Yet it took me a good few years to figure out that this was the part of the work I was already doing which a) I most enjoyed and b) held the most value for my clients, because I do it in a way nobody else does. During those pre-lightbulb moment years I worked with some really cool businesses. I helped them find their voice, reach new audiences and ultimately, sell more stuff.

Things were good, for several years. My work gave me freedom, I travelled whenever and wherever I wanted, I met some great people. There were successes to celebrate and failures to learn from. Some of the time I really enjoyed my work. But after a while I didn't, and I wasn't sure exactly why.

Until one day I realised I was basically following someone else's rules in almost every aspect of my biz. Those useful best practices and tools of the trade we're supposed to follow at the outset – with good reason – had become so embedded that they'd taken over. I'd somehow reached a point where there wasn't much of me left in my work or the way I marketed it (ironic, I know). I was just a copywriter, like many others. Nothing wrong with that in itself, but it just wasn't how I saw myself when I closed my laptop and left work at the end of the day. I'd become reluctant, even afraid, to run my business the way I really wanted to. Instead, I was doing it the way I felt I was expected to. This impacted so much of what I was doing: the hours I worked, the people I worked with, the way I communicated with them, the fees I charged and ultimately, the way I felt about who I was and what I was doing.

So I stopped. I tried looking at my work with a new perspective. And that was when I had a kind of breakthrough. I realised there were some parts of my work that I just didn't enjoy doing, so I stopped doing them. And I started to focus more on the parts which I did enjoy, and which clients seemed to appreciate. It sounds ridiculously simple to me now, but it can be a hard lesson to learn for many people. Yet it's really just a question of perspective.

So, this is what I want to share with you: When you're in business for yourself, perspective is everything. It may seem like you're supposed to always do things a particular way, because that's what Tony Guru says, and he wrote the book on it – but that's just one perspective. It may seem like you should be worrying about something in your work while you're eating dinner – an email you sent a client, or a creative decision you made that day – but that's just one perspective. It may seem, when you notice your work shifting in a new direction, like you're drifting further away from what you set out to do, but that's just one perspective. Perhaps you're actually moving closer to what you SHOULD be doing... for now.

This is one of the most important things I've learned over the past decade since I quit my last job (no, I didn't punch any bosses, but I thought about it more than once): When you commit to doing something in your business – like creating a service, choosing a niche, creating a marketing plan – do it wholeheartedly. But understand that at some point in the future, it's ok to walk away from that commitment and do something else.

I used to give myself such a hard time about sticking to one plan, about defining myself as the thing that I was doing at that time. But after years of seeing other smart, happy, creative biz-owners making sharp turns in different directions and thriving, I finally recognised that actually, it's ok to change direction now and again. Lots of entrepreneurs and freelancers were already doing this, of course. I would see people I remem-

ber being just copywriters or designers or photographers a couple of years ago now doing (and talking about) completely different things. Some of them would even switch gears in their
business twice, and I noticed that it didn't kill them (because I
was still getting their emails).

So I gave myself permission to try different directions too.
To try ideas on and see what fit. To experiment more. I mean,
if running your own business isn't just one long experiment, I
don't know what is. But YOU need to give yourself permission
to do that. Don't wait for it from anyone else.

I changed my positioning, my processes, my niche, my
schedule. Not all at once, it just kind of evolved. Until eventually, I found a combination that worked for me. By the time
you read this, it will probably have changed again. And these
days, I'm ok with that. It's just a question of perspective.

So if you feel like you want to do more of the things you
enjoy, to ditch the things you don't enjoy, to make up your own
title for what you do, or just to continue without a fully-
defined title for a while, go ahead. You're in charge. Nothing is
permanent. Have some fun. And remember: you are not your
business. But it is a part of you. Now, go get 'em.

One Step

Sue Heatherington (UK)

This step.
The little one just in front of you.
Breathe.
It's yours to take

We often tell ourselves that we need to do
something significant and meaningful
to feel like we're making progress.
Yet every movement begins with the first step.
We don't have to make it big.

About Ian Berry

Since 1990 Ian Berry has worked as a mentor for more than 1000 leaders, women and men, in over 40 countries. He helps purpose-driven business owners and leaders, executives in corporations, and professional service providers to see, unearth, magnify and enhance their essence (unique personal wisdom).

The author of Heart-Leadership Become the Wise Leader You Want to Be, and Changing What's Normal, Ian is a student and teacher of elevating tough-mindedness, tender-heartedness, trustworthiness, truth-telling, and tolerance as the essential 21st century leadership behaviours.

Ian also helps to escalate genuine business collaboration and leadership in overcoming society challenges, and engineering best business results at the least personal costs.

A conversationalist, speaker and mentor, Ian hosts online events every month for small groups of leaders.

Ian is also the host of We Need To Talk where stories that stir hearts and shift thinking are told and heard, and where life-enhancing sparkenation conversations ensue.

The founder of Wise Leaders Community Ian leads and co-leads peer groups online and in person that are dedicated to advancing and supporting the practice of wise leadership. Ian is also the creator and facilitator of The Wise Leaders Workshop.

Meet Ian at:
https://www.ianberry.biz/
https://twitter.com/ianberry1
https://www.linkedin.com/in/ianberry1/
https://www.facebook.com/IanBerryBusinessMentor/

Don't Die with Your Music Locked in You

Ian Berry (Australia)

*Our life's work, our reason for being, is found at the
intersection between can do, will do, love to do,
and people who love what I do.*

I was born with a small birthmark about the size of my little fingernail, on the inside of my right knee. I scratched it a few times playing sports and would just put a band-aid or bandage on it. I never thought much about it until it grew bigger in my twenty-first year. I went to see a doctor who removed it in day surgery a few hours later. I drove home not thinking much of it. He was later to tell me that it was a melanoma and not to worry that they had got it all. I was left with a nasty scar as a reminder. This particular doctor never told me anything about how serious melanoma can be.

Then in my twenty-third year I noticed a hard lump about the size of a cricket ball in my right groin. My wife was pregnant with our daughter Jessica at the time. We did not know then whether we were having a girl or a boy. We went to see Dr. Lionel Neri, a renowned surgeon recommended by our GP. After many tests and conversations he told us it was a melanoma and that I needed to have an operation to remove the lump and several lymph nodes. He told us that the survival rate was one in five and that he would do his best. He then stunned us by suggesting that my attitude would be a key to my survival. I vividly remember our son Lukas, who was eighteen months old, running around the room without a care in the world while Dr. Neri was giving us news that really took our breath away.

Dr. Neri suggested a mantra and to say it out loud in front of a mirror: "*I have an attitude of gratitude*". I didn't understand it then yet I dutifully followed his suggestion in front of a mirror, three times a day, before the operation. I knew nothing then of the heart-mind connection, or about meditation, which Dr. Neri taught me, or about affirmations or anything of this nature. I have been speaking the words out loud three times a day ever since. I've learned that when we are grateful for what we've got we are much more appreciative of more that comes our way.

Dr. Neri came to see Carol and me on the day I could finally go home, after weeks in hospital. His parting words were, "*Don't die with your music locked in you.*" Carol and I had no idea what he meant! Simply being alive was enough for us then. We later learned that music was a metaphor for essence (our unique personal wisdom).

Later still we discovered that the expression "*most people die with their music locked in them*" originated from the British Prime Minister Benjamin Disraeli who probably borrowed from the following words by Oliver Wendell Holmes. Sr. "*A few can touch the magic string, and noisy fame is proud to win them: Alas for those that never sing, but die with all their music in them.*"

I began to take my essence seriously. I became passionate about my essence and the essences of other people. I gradually began to notice the nuances in people. I became curious and committed to understanding myself and other people as fully as possible. These discoveries were the beginning of what has become my life's work – to inspire people to find their voice, sing their song, play their music and for them to inspire others to do the same.

Unearthing your essence pathway one

I've developed three key ways to unearth your essence. The first is to use music as an acronym to learn what is enough for you in five critical areas. For me enough means sufficient. I am grateful to Lynne Twist for this insight in her great book, **The Soul of Money**.

- Meaning.
- Unusual.
- Special.
- Inspirational.
- Curiosity.

I suggest contemplating this question over several days, *"What brings you sufficient meaning in your life?"* Then answer, *"What is unusual about me?"* Follow this with making a list of all the things that make you feel special about yourself. Next write down the one thing that other people have told you is inspirational about you. Finally note over several days what makes you curious.

A second pathway to unearth your essence is to answer the question, *"What makes my heart sing?"* Stories and conversations make my heart sing. I continue, despite decades of experience, to hone my story telling skills as well as my skills in having candid, convivial, compassionate, conscious and compelling conversations. Stories and conversations enrich the relationships essential to help us to turn possibility into reality. A combination of stories (yours and mine) that stir hearts and shift thinking lead to life-enhancing conversations. From such stories and conversations come defining moments for people and for me. My heart sings every time I experience an aha moment or when I am privileged to witness someone else's aha moment.

My heart sings through reading books and researching and writing my own books. I'm called to dig deeper, to find out, to learn, and to discover wisdom that can benefit humanity. What makes your heart sing? My heart sings when, through respectful dialogue and debate, people reach a shared-view about the way forward together.My heart sings when I'm able to create and co-create processes that help people to see, unearth, magnify and enhance their essence and the essence of other people. My heart sings when I'm able to create and co-create processes that make it simple for people to bring their essence to their work. My heart sings when I am able to help people to make more meaning in their life and to keep meaningful progress visible. What makes your heart sing?

A third pathway to unearth your essence is to create a one page Career and Life-Calling Card. I am very grateful to the works of Joseph Campbell, Ken Robinson, Steven Farber, Daniel Pink, and Hector Garcia and Francesc Miralles for their work in the area of vocation / work / mission / purpose that has helped me to develop the career and life-calling card. You'll find their books listed in the notes at the end of this chapter.

The concept of *"follow your bliss"* comes from Joseph Campbell in his book **Hero of a Thousand Faces**. It has resonated with me since I first read the book over 30 years ago. The very best explanation that I have ever come across for follow your bliss comes from the film **Finding Joe**, which is a documentary about Joseph Campbell's work. In the film the President of the Joseph Campbell Foundation describes bliss as "*doing what you can't not do.*" I love this! It is a wonderful way to describe essence.

In his excellent book, **The Element – how finding your passion changes everything**, Ken Robinson says about the element "*the place where the things we love to do and the things we are good at come together.*"

"*Do what you love, in the service of people who love what you do,*" from **The Radical Leap** by Steven Farber, is perhaps my favourite line of all time when it comes to meaningful work.

What drives us according to Daniel Pink in his books, **A Whole New Mind and Drive – the surprising truth about what motivates us,** are the three factors below:

- Autonomy: the urge to direct our own lives
- Mastery: the desire to get better and better at something that matters
- Purpose: the yearning to do what we do in the service of something larger than ourselves

The Japanese say everyone has an ikigai. The French call it raison d'être. In their beautiful book **Ikigai The Japanese Secret to a Long and Happy Life**, Hector Garcia and Francesc Miralles quote from people born in Okinawa, the island with the most centenarians in the world – "*our ikigai is the reason we get up in the morning.*"

From all of these works and my own experience in working with people to find their essence, I conclude that our life's work, our reason for being, is found at the intersection between can do, will do, love to do, and people who love what we do.

I recommend creating a one-page visual as a key heart and head action. Call it Career and Life-Calling Card and feature your answers to the following questions:

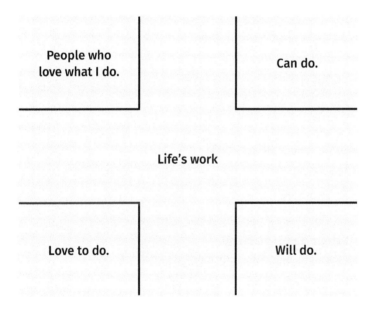

People who love what I do.

Can do.

Life's work

Love to do.

Will do.

Can Do

- What do I know?
- What are my key skills?
- What is my real expertise?
- How do I practice what I know?

Will do

- What is my attitude to living?
- What am I really committed to?
- How can I be more disciplined in taking action?
- How am I really different from others who do what I do?

Love to do

- My purpose in life is?
- What Am I passionate about?
- I find Joy in?
- My art is?
- My essence is?

People who love what I do

- How do I:
- Serve others?
- Help people achieve what is important to them?
- Solve people's problems?
- Offer solutions to people's challenges?
- Exchange value with other people?
- Deliver value to other people?

When we have unearthed and seen clearly our essence, and then dedicated ourselves to magnifying and enhancing it, we have unlocked our value. This is a key to how we show up in the world and how we make the difference we are inspired to make. Whatever your life's work you will receive enough for you according to how much you feel valued and how well you exchange and deliver value.

Forty-four years on from first hearing the phrase *"Don't die with your music locked in you"* I can say without any doubt that finding my music (my essence) and helping others to do the same has enabled me to achieve sufficiency in the areas of life that are important to me.

I recommend that, as you unlock your music, you notice what is enough for you in the most important areas of your life. For me three areas really matter. First, discretionary time. I have learned that having such is true wealth. Second is making sure that I have the energy to do what brings me joy. Third is feeling valued and helping others to feel valued. I get great inspiration and encouragement from these Brene Brown words (download them yourself via the link in the notes. *"No matter what gets done and how much is left undone, I am enough. It's going to bed at night thinking, yes, I am imperfect and vulnerable and some-times afraid, but that doesn't change the truth that I am also brave and worthy of love and belonging."* (Brene Brown, **The Gifts of Imperfection** 10th Anniversary edition)

Who will you become? What will you do next? Unlock your music and let us all sing together.

References

The Hero with a Thousand Faces, Pantheon Books, 1949, Joseph Campbell.

The Radical Leap, Dearborn Trade Publishing, 2004, Steve Farber.

'Ikigai The Japanese Secret to a Long and Happy Life', Hutchinson, 2017, Hector Garcia and Francesc Miralles,

Drive – the surprising truth about what motivates us, Canongate, 2010, Daniel Pink.

The Element, Penguin Books, 2009, Ken Robinson.

https://brenebrown.com/tgoi-downloads/

This Day

Sue Heatherington (UK)

Today
I am.
My whole life,
like rings
in a tree.

Today,
you are
wonderfully you.
No more,
no less,
complete.

This day
we are
gifts.

About Darcy Lee

Darcy Lee has made handbags, jewelry and accessories for the home within a light manufacturing environment and then owned a small gift shop called Heartfelt in San Francisco from 1999-2019. She is the mom of a daughter and step mom to a son and daughter. They light up her life. Recently she has started a subscription box called Hail the Snail Mail which encourages connection through writing letters and sending mail. She loves connection, clothes and community.

Meet Darcy at:
https://heartfeltsf.com
https://www.instagram.com/heartfeltsf/
https://www.facebook.com/HeartfeltSF
https://www.linkedin.com/in/darcy-lee-62b29214/

A Golden Break

Darcy Lee (USA)

How a poignant encounter helped me realize that helping and listening to others was the best route to a meaningful life in which I was more than enough.

I broke once, as a fragile teacup breaks, cup and saucer wholly shattered.

As I prepared to write this chapter, I felt myself holding back. I listened to Glennon Doyle and Abby Wambach recently on Krista Tippet's podcast, **On Being**, and they mentioned that life is like a series of nesting dolls, that it is vital to get to the inner one, the one that scares you because that one holds you back. In preparation for this chapter, I have turned to every bright shiny object that I could to keep the dolls nested, protected, and not exposed.

I have gone to the same therapist for many years, so I asked her what I could write about for this book. My therapist is named Beth: she did not hesitate. She said, "*Tell about when you broke and then had a vision for what you wanted. You have the rare capacity for making the impossible happen.*" It gave me chills when she said that.

My break came on suddenly; I started to wake up in the morning undone, with severe anxiety and nausea. I had known anxiety attacks since I was small, they started early. When we got dressed up to go downtown, I would start to tremble. I'd ask my mom if we could not go in elevators. She knew this territory; she called them nervous spells. Now I appreciate all the tools I use to fight this physiology, but back then she had none. A mother of two in the 1950s and '60s had little access to therapy or remedies aside from shame and hiding. She would choose stores with escalators, and I learned early how to work around anxiety, rather than calm it.

But these spells rocketed into my life in my early 40's. This time they felt different. If elevators were my first avoidance spot, it was as if I woke up in an imaginary one and at a complete loss how to open the door or get to the main floor.

I owned a business with another woman; I was the designer of items for the home. We had an incredible factory workspace in San Francisco flooded with light and a view of the Bay Bridge. At the height of our busy season, we had 20-30 staff people busily making things. I managed the people and the creative part. My friend handled all our sales. I loved what I did; figuring out how to make stuff within a light manufacturing environment was dreamy. I don't think I focused too much on my heart's calling or what I was giving to the world, the treadmill moved too quickly. Trade shows, deadlines, big orders, reps, seasonal colors, profit, it was all part of the process.

And then it stopped, my body screamed out; within months of my symptoms starting, I dropped 40 pounds off my 5'10 frame. I was sitting at the end of a very dark tunnel. Scenes flash by now from that time. An endocrinologist said my cortisol level was the highest he had ever measured; my regular doctor said Prozac was the answer (I later found out her husband was a pharmaceutical salesperson). Trips to the emergency room and visits to doctors who looked at me with sympathetic yet unknowing eyes. My 6-year-old daughter stood by my bedside and asked if I was going to die. I was not leaving the house; a simple trip to the grocery store, a few blocks away felt unsurmountable.

During this dark time, I sought a therapist. Friends recommended Beth, the woman who brought me to this story. She had recently moved across the street from me. I could crawl to her office. We began. I reflect now on my support system, the friends that rang my doorbell, my husband (totally baffled but there for me), the endless calls I made to doctors, the questions I asked.

A stranger who had heard of my plight telephoned out of the blue. They knew of a woman who treated women over 40 with sudden onset debilitating anxiety. I was more than intrigued. She was a scientist, a brain chemist who worked with a doctor in Aspen, Colorado. I thanked the caller profusely and called Dr. Bronson. She answered the phone and made immediate suggestions. Her demeanor was firm and confident; she said she could help me. She suspected it was a hormonal imbalance causing my symptoms, and she recommended a regime.

I booked an appointment to see her in Aspen. My 95-pound self got on an airplane with my husband. She met with me for two days straight. The tests she ordered confirmed her suspicions, and she zoomed ahead. I did everything she recommended and slowly found my appetite. My body and mind returned as quickly as they had left me.

But my business partner and I wanted to move on. I had taken on the role of child within our work environment, and she was the grown up. I had become dependent on her business sense and nothing about that worked for me anymore. We put our business up for sale. The business sold.

I was also struggling within my marriage. I began to assert myself within my husband's extreme demands.

As Beth saw me start to recover and witnessed all this change, she asked me to do an exercise: if I could dream and do anything I wanted, what would it be? I closed my eyes; I wanted a store, a community center where I could sell things I made and show up for people. I wanted to share my taste and whimsy. I wanted a change. I dreamed of flying bagels in from New York City and a line out the door for them. The bagels never happened, but the line out the door often did.

A store in my neighborhood named Heartfelt came up for sale a few months after my dream exercise. I bought the name and the contents of a small storefront.

I was learning and thriving. It was as if I had found a place in which I felt enough. My marriage was not thriving, and it ended at the same time as an opportunity to buy the building that housed Heartfelt came up.

The feeling of I am enough, this is working would make fleeting appearances but duck back when confronted with what now seem like mundane stereotypes. I applied for an SBA (Small Business Administration) loan to purchase the building, and I found myself in the bank office with four male loan officers and my SBA representative (a woman). I was going through the divorce at the time, and the description, a single divorced woman on the loan papers, was jarring, especially to the loan officers.

They questioned me at length, and I was unsure whether to portray myself as a lovely damsel in distress or a competent, well-dressed businesswoman. I could feel myself flipping between the two. I cringe thinking of it now. Where am I in this transaction? Am I enough to pull this off? I knew that a woman with clear evidence of profit and loss statements in the black was insufficient, and I struggled with how else to prove that I could purchase this building and pay the mortgage with ease from my successful store. Somehow, they approved my loan.

Now I was a store owner and a building owner, and a whole new menu of I am not enough was surfacing. I am just bringing stuff into the world, what a waste! I volunteered to make the neighborhood more vital. I became president of the merchants' association, communicated with the police and the mayor's office to make our neighborhood better for everyone. I developed constant negative chatter that I was not contributing as much as a nurse or a teacher and yet I loved my job. I loved creating a place where you could let your imagination run wild, a unique store with a wide array of things that somehow did not make sense and yet did.

And then a chilly winter day, with me behind the glass counter, changed everything. A family came in; a couple with their young adult daughter. They looked and looked; they were so careful and quiet. After an hour, they brought a few things up to the counter. I made small talk, and then the mother spoke, "*We are in the neighborhood because our son passed away in a ski accident a few months ago. We are here to clear out his apartment. This was his favorite place. We wanted to experience your shop.*" We all teared up together. I had a moment of clarity, that all the years of listening and helping and interacting with people had meaning. And I realized we were more than enough at that moment.

After 20 years I closed the shop, it was holiday time 2018 and I came home and said, "This is the last year", I wanted to end it with love and energy and the energy was waning. The world was gift shopping in a different way and slowly the numbers started to reflect that. The store closed in August 2019. We are not always aware of what we give; during the last few months, my customers expressed sentiments of love and gratitude that I'd had no idea they felt. Yet the trio in the chilly months from years ago are the ones that changed me forever. And I am blessed to have talked to countless women who, launched into perimenopause the way I had been, found their way to me. Showing up with my heart is the most fulfilling thing of all. I found myself on a path I could never have imagined.

At the end of that podcast **On Being**, the three strong women speaking concluded that courage is born of pain, waiting, and rising. Feeling the fear and not letting it stop you is where the gold lies; you are more than enough.

Fishermen

Caroline Harvey (Spain)

How many times have I wandered past
The fishermen on the beach?
Too many to count.
How many fish have I seen reeled in?
Not one.
And yet there they are at dusk, all set up in a row
Like soldiers, waiting.
They don't seem to chat,
Each too busy in their familiar fishing ritual.
Now and again they adjust, remove,
Cast their lines afresh.
They seem happy.

About Joel Hughes

Joel runs Glass Mountains (est 2001), a WordPress design & support agency in the UK, with clients in the UK and North America.

Meet Joel at:
https://www.glassmountains.co.uk/
https://www.linkedin.com/in/joelhughes/
https://twitter.com/Joel_Hughes

Learning to Change

Joel Hughes (UK)

How my entrepreneurial struggles taught me not to be hard on myself, to allow myself to make mistakes, and to make sure I learn from them

I've always struggled with the concept of work. As a fresh-faced IT graduate, I worked for Amex as a junior programmer earning £19K a year and I just could not comprehend how what I did between 9 and 5:30 each day contributed to that salary! From that point on, a fascination sparked within me about the nature of work, how it should fit into our busy lives, how it dovetails with happiness – in short: what is enough?

The Y2K

On the run-up to the year 2000, the millennium Y2K bug allowed me to spread my wings from the traditional employment route and to instead work as an independent contractor. I earned very good money, but I still wasn't happy. It just wasn't very satisfying.

Then in late 1999, I was given the opportunity to work on a nascent website project. I found the whole technology fascinating and decided that this was what I was going to hang my career hat on going forward. I would carry on short term contracting but in the web technology sphere.

My New Problem

Everything was fine for a while, I enjoyed the web technology I was working with but the actual units of work were less fun. Working with companies for a short period of time, as a pure hired hand, I felt like I was not part of the decision-making process – I was simply being told what to do. This soon put me at a crossroads. I either went back as a full-time employee (which hopefully got me a seat at the table with the decision makers), or I completely restructured how I worked with clients. I no longer wanted to be a nameless hired hand, I wanted to be valued and listened to.

The Home Desk

In 2007 I remember sitting at my newly constructed and freshly laid out desk at home. The laptop was up and running. Pencils sharpened, notepad at the ready. It felt exhilarating and daunting. However, there was a problem, the phone did not ring. I had no work.

Network Issues

I had started my business with no network to speak of, and no real inclination of how to promote my services, and to get work. In hindsight, I think the self-confident rush of knowing that I was good at the technicalities of my job blinded me as to all the other skills I needed; e.g. marketing.

The first few years were tough. I'd come into it without the required well-rounded skills. Even better, we'd had our first child: a joyful event but one that heaps more pressure I think on the self-employed: am I working hard enough? Could I do better? Am I being a good father? Am I providing as best I can? Or am I being selfish in pursuing this career route?

The Early Years

The early years of business meant I took on any work that came my way, irrespective of whether it was a good fit for my business or not. Indeed, I don't think I had any idea of what good fit meant back then. If a work opportunity was presented to me, I assumed it simply was a puzzle to solve in terms of winning the work – and that the only positive outcome was to win the work. Oh have I changed my opinion on that!

This situation of take on any work carried on for years. Yes, I was wrong to do this but I am thankful in a way. This was a lived experience that, when you allow yourself to review it honestly, gave me strong pointers as to how actually I wanted to sail my business.

Changes

Many experiences shaped my business journey. For one, I worked with a really, really bad client. I don't mean they were personally bad – they were not. They were just a terrible fit for me. It was one of those where (especially early in your career) you look at the money on offer and get blinded by that. The person was nice, the project was interesting, but the money for this highly complex app was terrible (though I didn't realise it at the time). To cut a long story short, I did a great job of the project (the code was reviewed by a third party after we parted company and it got a glowing review). However, the whole project was a massive ball of stress. The project took way more hours and effort than I budgeted for – and the client never appreciated that (let alone compensated). They had no ability to compromise – and I was not skilled enough to negotiate.

I remember one particularly bad moment … My brother, his wife and two young children had flown over from France (where they live) to visit. They had come over to see the family in South Wales but I hardly saw any of them at all because of this nightmare project. I was constantly working on unrealistic deadlines, burning the midnight oil, meeting the client for reviews. Instead of spending time on day trips with my brother and his family, I was slogging away at the keyboard writing code for the ever-shifting sands of this scope creeping project.

The End of the Beginning

At the end of the holiday, I drove my brother and his family back to Bristol airport and waved them off. I got back to the car and, realising that I'd got my priorities completely wrong, I broke down in tears and sobbed. I'd hardly seen them! I'd not spent quality time with them. Instead, I'd wasted time trying to appease a client who was unappeasable – what a miserable waste of time.

I'm not much of a crier so this was a big event for me. It felt cathartic. A release of all the pent up stress. And I knew that something had to change. But what?

The Change

The big change for me was being much more selective about the clients who I work with. Work is very important to me. It's not all of me – but it is a huge part. And that huge part has to be fun and rewarding.

I began learning more about business, attending networking events, and reading business books. In short, expanding the horizons of my knowledge beyond the obvious boundaries of the technical skills required to design websites (in hindsight I wish I had done so sooner but there we go).

The Velvet Rope Policy

Michael Porter talks about the velvet rope policy – establishing criteria for people to work with you. Helping define and come to terms with the requirements that you set before you let people into your life.

This is critical. You have to take a stand here. Yes it is difficult when you need to bring work in and perhaps on occasion you may be slightly more lenient with your velvet rope policy but be careful. Poor fit clients take up too much space in your calendar and your brain and heart, space that could equally be filled by lovely, warm, rewarding clients (yes, they do exist!).

I would also say this, poor fit clients are seldom happy and will typically only ever be able to refer you to equally poor fit clients. Whilst good fit clients are a joy to work with and will automatically steer you to other good clients. Your work can become your greatest marketing asset – so invest in it by avoiding poor fit opportunities.

Is this Enough?

I love my job. I enjoy it. The business has grown from those early days and now I have a team to help manage all aspects of projects (note: when I first had the basics of a team, it was the most amazing joy being able to go on holiday and know that work was still happening and projects were still moving forward!).

My job has incredible flexibility – I work when I want to work. My team are fully remote (and have been for many years) – when COVID hit it was business as usual for how the company runs.

Is everything perfect? Of course not. Everything is fluid, and you need to be watchful. A key thing for me is to make sure I'm still enjoying things. If I'm doing tasks that I don't enjoy then why don't I enjoy them? Is it because I'm not the best person to do that task? If so, who needs to do it?

Closing Thoughts

If you are thinking of following your entrepreneurial dream then I wish you all the best of luck. If you take away one thing from my words here, let it be this: you are undoubtedly better prepared than I was for setting sail on the choppy seas of running a business! Don't be hard on yourself, allow yourself to make mistakes, just make sure you learn from them.

Enough for me is having money for the basics and a few treats, having time with my family, playing my guitar, and putting good work and goodwill out into the world. What is it for you?

A Little Note to Ourselves

Sue Heatherington (UK)

What do you want to hear?
Or rather, what do you know you need to hear?
What words need unlocking from inside,
that only your voice can utter?
And only your ears can hear ...
Whisper gently.
And be at rest from the chatter.

About Jacqueline Davis

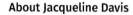

Jacqueline R Davis (Jackie) is a marketer and storyteller. She shares stories to inspire women to step into their greatness and be seen and heard. Her debut storytelling performance was on a live Zoom event hosted by GBH, a leader in public media. The program, Silver Linings: Stories from the Stage, was later recorded live from the stage and broadcast on television via WORLD Channel and the social media platforms YouTube, Facebook, Instagram, and Twitter.

A graduate of the Harvard Business School and Cornell University, Jackie held marketing positions at Fortune 500 companies, including Boston Scientific, Intel, HBO, and IBM.

Jackie's first entrepreneurial venture, RoomScape Interiors, was an award-winning residential interior design firm. For over nine years Jackie traveled across the United States redesigning rooms on HGTV's Decorating Cents. She shared decorating tips on cable television, in print publications and online. Her work appeared in the 2% Women of Color design exhibit at the American Institute of Architects Convention in 2008.

Jackie held leadership roles in social organizations and on Boards such as the HBS Women's Alumni Association, NCNW, and Massachusetts Coalition for the Homeless.

She resides in Massachusetts with her husband, but both still call New York home.

Meet Jacqueline at:
https://www.linkedin.com/in/jackierdavis
https://www.JackieDavis.me

Making Meaning is Key to Happiness

Jacqueline Davis (USA)

How I freed myself from the slavery of the almighty
dollar, broke the chains of the corporate workplace and stopped
tolerating the microaggressions of others.

I ran across Anderson Bridge to join the other 30,000 some odd people in Harvard Yard. I was out of breath when I took my seat among the sea of black robes and mortarboards for the official commencement ceremony. Before the dean called our school, I pulled out the dollar bill I'd so carefully folded and put in my pocket earlier that morning. I was ready.

Our school was next. Before the dean could confer our degrees, we jumped to our feet and roared. It was loud, raucous, boastful. I'm sure we were heard way across the river back to the Boston campus.

Unlike some schools where graduates threw their hats into the sky to celebrate the occasion, we waved dollar bills in the wind. Some classmates clutched bills in both hands. Was that Benjamin Franklin on their money? We were graduates of the Harvard Business School. Masters and mistresses of the universe. We were all going to be rich.

I envied my classmates who joined investment banks or consulting firms because they were making the BIG bucks. In retrospect, this was odd for me because I hadn't entered b-school to earn lots of money. I wanted to study marketing. By the time I graduated, I'd succumbed to peer pressure and outside expectations. My relationship with money changed. The more money I had, the better.

My career decisions were motivated by money. If the work was tolerable and the money was good, that was enough for me. I happily settled into my jobs and waited for the headhunter to call with the next opportunity to join a company at a bigger salary and more benefits.

I became a slave to the almighty dollar, chained to corporate workplaces where I tolerated microaggressions. Subtle insults and racial biases were directed against me as if intended to keep me in my place. It wasn't always apparent to other people when I was marginalized or ignored, but I could see it.

For example, I'd make a point in a meeting on more than one occasion, and it seemed to fall on deaf ears. A few minutes later, a white male would make the same comment. Not only was he heard, but coworkers remarked that his point was brilliant and insightful.

What had just happened? I could hardly believe my ears. I realized I had a choice. I could be silent, let it go, or I could speak up. So, I opened my mouth and said, *"Excuse me. I just made the same point."* My colleagues reacted with guilty stares as if they knew he stole my words, but they chose to ignore the theft. Sometimes they asked me if I was sure of what I said.

I felt as though they questioned my credibility. The fake ignorance infuriated me. I had to bite my tongue to keep from spewing hot, nasty words or risk getting labeled as the stereotypical angry Black woman. That would surely damage my reputation. But why was his voice heard and not mine?

Another memorable experience occurred after I joined a company through an acquisition. I'd participated in the launch of the first Computer Clubhouse. My new manager was pleased with my performance and supported my request to become a permanent member of a team. It was my opportunity to do challenging, creative work.

Unfortunately, his boss blocked my request. He explained that I had to move to the corporate headquarters located in California if I wanted more meaningful work. His reason didn't make any sense to me because I'd be traveling around the United States to open new Computer Clubhouse locations. What difference did it make where I lived? I never got a straight answer and didn't understand his motivations. Can I prove there was bias? No.

However, according to the McKinsey & Company study, Women in the Workplace 2020: "*Compared with their colleagues of other races and ethnicities, Black women have always had distinct, and by and large worse, experiences at work. They are promoted more slowly than other groups of employees and are significantly underrepresented in senior leadership. They are less likely than women of other races and ethnicities to say their manager advocates for new opportunities for them. And they have fewer interactions with senior leaders, which means they often don't get the sponsorship and advocacy they need to advance. Given these challenges, it's not surprising that Black women are less likely than employees of other races to report they have equal opportunity to advance at work.*"[1]

Occasionally, I even experienced slights from vendors. One vendor I'd communicated with via telephone and email was eager to meet with me. He had no idea what to expect when he came to the office because companies did not display employee photos on the internet yet. Two of my direct reports joined me in the meeting. They were both white, one male and the other female. The sales rep snapped his head around when we introduced ourselves. He looked shocked to learn that I, a Black woman, was the manager. It would have been funny if it wasn't so insulting.

The rep avoided eye contact with me and directed his attention and questions to the other people in the room. I had to take control of the situation and calmly but firmly informed the sales rep that I required answers to my questions before approving the purchase. The prospect of losing a sale got his attention. The whole tenor of the meeting changed, and he began to address me directly. It was clear that he understood I was the decision-maker he had to please if he wanted the business.

Finally, one day I looked at myself in the mirror and said, enough is enough. I was tired of the racist and sexist treatment I'd experienced at work. Some people are more adept at ignoring snubs and choose to stay in their corporate jobs for the money, the title, or the benefits. But, for me, there was no price tag on respect or being valued or heard. My employers couldn't pay me enough to remain invalidated or underemployed. My achievements proved I was capable and worthy of better career opportunities.

From early childhood, a network of supportive family members and friends valued me, reinforced my value in myself, and bolstered my confidence. Later in life, I sometimes found allies in coworkers, managers, and even vendors. And as for the naysayers, it was their issue, not mine, if they did not recognize my worth. I didn't need to prove that I am enough. But I realized no one was going to rescue me from an unfulfilling career. I had to save myself.

A few years before my 50th birthday, I created an escape plan to remove the golden handcuffs. I decided to pursue a dream and attended design school at night while I worked during the day. It took two years, but I finally squirreled away enough money to feel financially secure without the promise of a paycheck. I took a deep breath, quit my job, and opened a residential interior design business.

Running my business was one of the highlights of my career. I was the boss with the power to control my fate. I selected the vendors I wanted to do business with and the clients I wanted to serve. My energy soared because I was in the flow. When I was motivated solely by the money, I knew something was missing, but I chose to ignore the void. Now I enjoyed the creative freedom I rarely experienced in my corporate jobs. Powered by my passion, I designed rooms my clients loved and helped fulfill their dreams of a beautiful home.

Although I pivoted the business several times to meet new market demands and stay ahead of the competition, it was unsustainable due to a downturn in the economy. After 14 years, I closed the business and returned to corporate marketing jobs to rebuild my nest egg. I hummed along in a corporate job until the spring of 2020. I became one of the 9.5 million employees in the U.S. who lost their job due to the COVID-19 pandemic.

The daily grind of the job search and the pressure to pay bills started to take a toll on my mental health. After countless days watching mind-numbing television programs and eating huge portions of junk food, I had to make a change. Lucky for me, I found a fun distraction in a Story Skills Workshop.

In just six weeks, I wrote my first story. I described an experience I had when I attended a predominantly white school. I was the only Black student in my 5th-grade classroom. The story is about luck, race, belonging, and becoming. Sadly, the story is as relevant today in 2021 as it was in 1965.

Three months after I completed the workshop, I recited the story on a live Zoom call hosted by GBH, a local public broadcast company. Then I delivered it on stage. The story was recorded and later aired on television by WORLD Channel. I had no idea I had such a powerful story inside me or that it would resonate with so many people. Finally, I was seen and heard.

Releasing my story to the world has freed me to tell more stories and live a more authentic life. I've learned that the best stories capture the audience's attention and take them on a journey that evokes an emotional response. I hope the story of my journey to entrepreneurship inspires you to have the courage to transform your career and your life.

Over the years, I've asked myself, what is enough? Back when I stood waving my dollar bill at graduation, I would have easily said that money was the answer. But time has given me new experiences that changed my perspective. Today, as I reflect on my life, the question I ask is, Enough of what?

Money is only one answer. My bank account balance does not define me. I am rich in ways that money can't buy. I have enough when I have the freedom to create. I have enough when I am respected. I have enough when I am treated justly. Yes, money is still important to me, but it's no longer a big part of my identity. There's more to life than making money. Making meaning is key to my happiness. My goal is to do meaningful work and share stories that improve society.

Enough for me is about having the income to feel secure, to have experiences that make me happy, and to be able to share my good fortune with people I love and the causes I support. By these criteria, I'm rich, and that is my definition of a mistress of the universe.

So, while many of my friends head into retirement, I am reinventing myself once again. I'm off to start my next big adventure, and for now, that is enough. I'm reminded of a quote from Oprah Winfrey, *"Be thankful for what you have; you'll end up having more. If you concentrate on what you don't have, you will never, ever have enough."*[2]

You may have doubts as you consider entrepreneurship. That's normal. You're human and, it's scary to take risks. But ask yourself if your corporate job is giving you enough, according to how you define enough. I'm convinced that running your own business is worth the risk, even with all the ups and downs during the journey. Go for it!

References

(1) Women in the Workplace 2020, a 63-page report from LeanIn.org in partnership with McKinsey & Company. https://wiw-report.s3.amazonaws.com/Women_in_the_Workplace_2020.pdf

(2) Oprah's Lifeclass, 2012.

Two Quotes to Live by
Jeremy Deedes (UK)

Gandalf the Grey tells us
what to do with our time,
*'All we have to do is decide what to do with the
time that is given to us.'*

Whilst Maya Angelou tells us
how to spend our time,
*'My mission in life is not merely to survive,
but to thrive; and to do so with some passion,
some compassion, some humour, and some style.'*

Simply two great quotes to live by.

About Con Christeson

Con Christeson is a community/public/ mixed media artist from St. Louis Missouri USA. Not really a muralist but the Bureau of Enquiry is up on Cherokee St., and Vehicle/Destination/Imagination is at the Forest Park Metro Link Station. Not a trained photographer, but employs its immediacy/accessibility as a window on the world. Not scared of performance, she works with others to write scripts, imagine movement, and perform. As a serial collaborator who rarely works alone, she works WITH others who have complementary skills, supports/displays the work of others at Red Chair Studios with an artist CoLAB and mentoring process. Local, national, and global work inform her work on the street. Cons published book has the title *What Is … What If? Confronting and Configuring a Community Arts Practice.*

Meet Con:
http://conchristeson.us
https://www.linkedin.com/in/conchristeson/

Looking at Looking

Con Christeson (USA)

How doing it out of love, not fear, builds bridges,
breaches comfort zones, and creates connection.

In 1999, shortly after I finished a community arts training fellowship, I had a conversation with a social work colleague. He was running a shelter for homeless men and was about to implement, with a community partner, an innovative way for his clients to move from transitional to permanent housing. He described this alternative path in detail, and he referred to the men as people who live in the margins of society.

Immediately, I saw a piece of loose-leaf paper in my head … something we've all used hundreds of times. A single sheet, with the blue horizontal lines. And that red line on the far left, running vertically from top to bottom. Imagine this common commodity as a metaphor, as a map. The flat blue lines are where most of us tend to travel. We write in our choices and keep track of our resources. We might even have an eraser to make changes. In the long blue line territory, we have options. We know we can get disoriented, destabilized, displaced by any number of things, but, with our resources, we manage to level out and carry on.

If we do cross over the red line, it firmly marks a whole other territory, thin as it is. Yes, the blue lines are there, but they are shorter. There is less room to make notes, stay steady. And then of course, there are the holes. Yup, holes. Multiple hazards in this

Sit. hear. see.

tight space. Navigation is difficult. If you bump into someone, trip over something, it could spell disaster. The constant vigilance is exhausting and downright disconcerting.

People who become homeless often find themselves stuck in the margin. My friend and I designed our first community art project with this metaphor to support his program. With creativity, we began to push and pull on that red line. Paint and paper, writing and story, movement and music became our first spoken-word performance piece. It was titled **Footnotes: From the Margins.** Twenty years later, we are still realizing our voice.

Looking In

In 2017, I went to Italy to train with a mentor. Her co-creation methodology (Artway of Thinking) includes 130+ tools. At the core, there is a focus on knowledge of the self. When I told her that I was at a career crossroads and wanted to make some choices and changes, she prepared a sequential series of three of these exercises. They were designed to unsettle and then ground me in a new intention, a new direction.

I was – and still am – intimidated by her energy and presence in general, and there are cultural challenges that exist in particular. The first day and the first two exercises were more than frustrating. I could not seem to meet her expectations satisfactorily. I learned that I am somewhat smug and surface about what I think I know and more than a little impatient with details … sigh.

She introduced the third exercise on the second day. It is called **My City of Opportunity.** The first step is the prep work, the mindset, the research in the form of deep reflection. Make lists in the categories of personal knowledge, relationships, resources, and perceived potential. Consider feelings, actions, and energies along with facts and information.

While I prepared the above, she printed out a Google map of St. Louis and taped it in four sections on the wall in front of me.I sat at a big table where there was a length of white paper and an assortment of markers and paint. My task was to transfer all or part of the map to the paper based on my lists and reflections. I would then attempt to identify known resources in my community and see new connections. And, as the final act of imagination: rename, recombine, reconnect the places on the map using words, pictures, and color to illustrate a new way of seeing, elipse a transformation.

The overwhelm from the previous day settled in my stomach. I tried to push it aside and continued the mapping exercise over the next few hours.She walked in and out of the room (distracting). She was supportive but critical (sobering). She was a little impatient at my attention to too much detail, and finally, she stopped and said, *"Play!Just play!"* before she walked away. (OK. Fine! I will!) Something gave, a blockage was removed.

All the prep work that I had done brought in the people and places and days of my life. They seemed to line up behind me to watch.I got a little silly. My pens began to record direction and destinations in words that surprised me. I travelled the roads and paths of where I go often, and happily named where I might go. She came back as our time was running out. She said, *"Now you've got it! Keep going ... I will add the colors for you."* Her paint, my pen finished the map that day, and the journey continues. When I look at it, even now, I see things that have become apart of my story.

That map has travelled with me. Its aesthetic is more than its plain paper and glue. It is my art, in pen and paint, held together with tape on paper. I used it to inspire students in Europe, talk to colleagues at national conferences, and interact with passersby on the street at the studio. It helps me tell my story. A record of where and whom and why. The thin red line on the loose-leaf paper has morphed into a flexible red thread that runs through-between-around people, places, and projects. That thread is my path, the lifeline of everyday consciousness, the sit/hear/see connections that run through community and culture.

Looking With

The Economy of the Everyday is the working title of my second book. That book will be an updated mapping of the margins and the main streets. Old tools sharpened for a new re-search. The goal is to engage creatively, document journeys, and share stories in the neighborhood, the city, the world, and back again. What will we find to count, save, connect, solve? Does our dailiness influence our interactions and intentions and how?

The Economy of the Everyday. Mine. Yours. Ours. Literal and physical maps to pore over together and alone. This is the business, the venture, the adventure. The red thread tethers and

extends. Local / national / global. Building bridges, breaching comfort zones, bids for connection made and accepted. Travel currency (necessary for transport and lodging, supplies and venues) might be generated peripherally with odd jobs and side gigs, grants, book tours, teaching. It may be generative with sales and fees from writing, speaking, consulting.

The age of COVID taught in many ways that the power of SOCIAL capital is not to be underestimated.

This investment comes with these dividends:

- To FIND the others
- To identify a direction WITH others
- To engage infinitely renewable, mutually bankable, spendable RELATIONSHIPS.

These ideas, these words influence our collective incomes and outcomes. If we choose this mindset, we can continue to make new sections of a common map, overlap into friendly territories, and realize fields of dreams.

In the age of COVID, regardless of location or status or ability:

- We learned a little or a lot.
- We coped well or badly.
- We made choices. Or not.

Online platforms (like **the Right Company**) were the drivers and monitors for many of us. It was exhausting and invigorating and maddening because we had to figure it out in real time with an impromptu team and an audience of strangers. We generated surprise and interest and movement. And we set ourselves up for a whole new round of post-COVID choices. How about that new website? You want to write a book? Can you design a course for the new market place? Do you quit? Down-size? Reconfigure? Is there a desk in a tall building that you might only visit occasionally but not exclusively?

What is LOVE in the age of COVID? Social justice? Climate justice? Equity and inclusion? The LUXURY of the time? The space to hear and be heard? The intention to consider? Re-consider? In real time?

Consider this: If you could design and implement a remote control mechanism, what would it look like? Consider the shape, the function, and the direction in which you would point it. Consider also how many buttons it would have / need, and how would they be labeled? Is a set of directions or caveats

8.

Go in.
find
out.

necessary? What priorities does it address for you? What is the story it tells about you?

I've given this journal assignment to students in communications classes over many years. They shared those journals with each other, and I've saved the best ones. There was one year, in two separate classes, that two students, unbeknownst to each other, responded almost identically. Their remotes only had two buttons. A down-facing arrow labeled fear. An arrow pointing up labeled love.

The directions were simple:
If you are not doing it out of love, you are doing it out of fear.
If you are not doing it out of love, you are doing it out of fear.

I contend that this can be applied to just about everything. Then, now, and beyond. It's a fundamental orientation that is available and workable. It will tell us when we are enough, when we have enough, what is enough. If you are not doing it out of love, you are doing it out of fear.

Make that map, and proceed accordingly. Amen.

Expanding our Sense of Personhood

Sue Heatherington (UK)

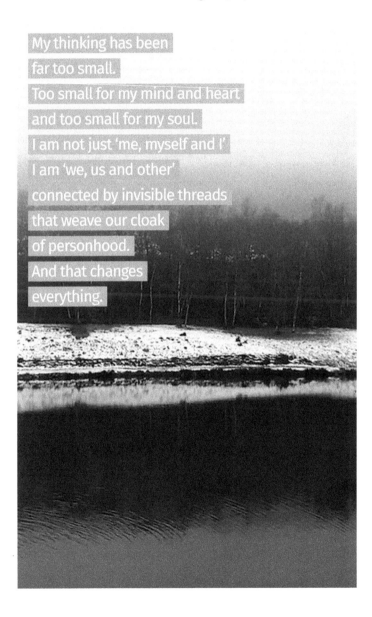

My thinking has been
far too small.
Too small for my mind and heart
and too small for my soul.
I am not just 'me, myself and I'
I am 'we, us and other'
connected by invisible threads
that weave our cloak
of personhood.
And that changes
everything.

About Ulla Raaf

Ulla remembers suffering as a child, when her concerns would not be understood, and her actions would be criticized or even punished. Becoming a mother she was confronted with similar issues again. Her deep wish to have a loving relationship with her daughter led her on the path to her final realization: When people feel understood, when they feel listened to and when they recognize another person's willingness to show interest, possibilities come up that you couldn't have dreamed of, like rewarding relationships, exceptional leadership, productive teams and supportive communities.

This was the basis for her brand „Logosynergie – comprehension connects". Identifying common ground and listening, leading to understanding and connection.

As an author and designer she creates books and media that help people discover and enhance their compassionate capabilities. In her key-note-speeches she points out the different aspects that lead to misunderstanding. For years she has been consulting, coaching and training mainly small companies and educational institutions. It is her belief that small has a lot of potential and she prefers working with people instead of organizations.

Ulla is trained as Empathic Coach®, Trainer for Nonviolent Communication, System Constellation Leader, Psychological Counsellor and Family Therapist, NLP Business Master and has graduated with a Diploma in Graphic Design.

Meet Ulla at:
https://ullaraaf.com
https://www.facebook.com/ulla.raaf
https://www.linkedin.com/in/ulla-raaf-531206206/
https://www.xing.com/profile/Ulla_Raaf/cv

Enough Time

Ulla Raaf (Germany)

When I slow down and use the time for myself,
it always feels similar to giving myself a present.

Have you ever considered how you are in relationship to
time? You might feel like you never have enough time or are
unable to take time for yourself. As a result you could think of
your work schedule as being in conflict with the time you have.
You might be forcing things because of time.

Valuing Time

Ever since starting my business career, I wondered why
people would boast about having so much to do, being so
stressed, and having absolutely no time. It never made any
sense to me. Some suggested that having too much time on my
hands could only mean that I was not successful. I was so em-
barrassed that I decided not to talk anymore about having
enough time.

Nevertheless, I never stopped questioning why I should
push myself so hard if this would result in having no time. So
by now, you might have already guessed that I value time over
many things like money, power, status, fame, praise, and approval. Love, friendship, a sense of personal satisfaction, and
having time are of utmost importance to me.

In hindsight, I sometimes wonder how I managed everything and still had time to spend. Being left as a widow with a
three-year-old, and a business with a six-figure debt and a
pending reboot due to a recession, wasn't easy at all and it didn't
seem like time for myself could ever be the most important

priority. Maybe my ingrained belief that after every low, a high will follow helped me. Add to that my ability to focus on what I'm doing one at a time and so intensely that I can get things done much quicker. Interruptions are what make it challenging to get things done on time.

How do you manage your day, the available hours, or the whole week? Taking or making time for yourself is valuable, a great luxury, and no flaw at all. Constantly being alert and stressed only causes burn-out or other illnesses in the long run.

Throwing away the alarm clock

I believe that we all have an internal clock. I perform best from about 8 am to 10 pm. I have often admired people who are able to be active in the middle of the night. For me, this has always been quite tough.

But then I started dancing as a hobby. Parties only started after 10 pm, so to participate, something had to change for me. I tried – successfully – to push my internal clock, and for some time, I was even able to perform until 2 – 3 am. During the pandemic, my internal clock quite quickly returned to its original times even though I by then had changed my biorhythm for nearly ten years.

One of the most important things I gift myself with is not to be awakened by an alarm clock. I love to start my day in my time. Sometimes this will be earlier, sometimes later. But it will be when I feel ready to get up. I would despise having an alarm clock waking me to morning yoga, writing morning pages, or going for morning walks – as often suggested – way before I'm ready for that. Don't get me wrong: I like starting mornings with these, only I wouldn't start the day way earlier than my biorhythm suggests to do so. If I do something, it must fit in my typical day.

The point of all this is to suggest to you to find out when you perform best. How does your internal clock tick? What can you do to serve your biorhythm? What keeps you from doing so?

Big chunks or small pieces

People working in companies seldom have the luxury to decide for themselves when and how long to work. Yes, there might be core times allowing employees to determine when to begin and end, but they only provide a relatively small amount of flexibility.

Being self-employed allows me the luxury of having a different way to use my time. My personal favorite is to work in small pieces. I start working for some time, then I stop and do something completely different. Of course, this only works so well because my office is at home. But I have noticed that I'm much more productive with this working style than I might be if working according to the clock. I am unsure if one can produce more valuable work by working in big chunks, like eight hours a day, only interrupted by some small breaks.

Have you ever thought about your way of working? What would you choose, if you could? What would be different? How would you organize your working hours best?

Letting Go

In a coaching session about having more time, a client once wrote each of her daily tasks on a piece of paper and put them all out on the floor to get the bigger picture. She also added the estimated time she would need for each task. In bird's-eye-view, she got an excellent impression of her choices. It was pretty clear that continuing the way she had until now would make gaining more time impossible. But she couldn't think of anything she might let go of or delegate to somebody else.

Have you ever thought about taking a sharp look at your daily tasks in this way? And to be critical about everything you want to keep in your schedule? Why can't you possibly let these things go? How come some things seem unavoidable? Do you gain something by doing or keeping a task? Who could help you? What would happen if the outcome was not exactly how you imagined? If you could do something differently, what would it be? Is the price you are paying for insisting on things being done a certain way worth paying?

What are the three most important things you spend your time on? Do you spend most of your time doing activities or with the people you love most? The people I've asked this question to mainly mentioned family, friends, and work as the three most essential things.

Spending Time and Slowing Down

Convenience is quite often the motivational factor for doing things the way we do. We believe we are making things easier. We tend to look for shortcuts, avoid any effort, choose fast food, and prefer using the car before going on foot or cycling. But how do we use the time we seem to gain by acting like this? Are we killing time with TV, Netflix, Social Media, video games? Or are we using our precious time for something valuable? Do we even know what would be beneficial to us?

When I use time for myself, it always feels similar to giving myself a present. I love cooking exquisite meals only for myself. I love playing my hand-pan, discovering new rhythms, based on the possibility to compose. I love going for long walks with my dog. Very often, my mind unconsciously uses those times to think about something challenging me. The positive effect is that more often than not, solutions pop up that I'd never thought about before. It seems to confirm the eureka effect.

Do you catch yourself simply killing time? How could you spend time being nice to yourself? What reenergizes you?

Children are excellent role models when dealing with time. They can't do what we adults believe we can. And they are right. Their concept of time is much more helpful for their well-being.

But I understand the parents, too. They often can't help being pressed into such a tight schedule so they desperately need creative ways to deal with time. As a mother, I admit falling into the time trap myself. But at some point, I was done with this and started improving my way of handling time. It began with the already mentioned method of segmenting my day in ways that fit me.

The next thing was not taking more jobs than I could easily handle while still having time for other things. It is very compelling to say yes to every offer, but it's pretty hard to get out once you are on the treadmill.

When you try to rush things they never get done faster. I've found the opposite to be true. When taking more time, I avoid mistakes. When thinking things through more thoroughly, plans get better. Going slow helps to avoid missing important details. How can you choose to spend your time? Can you think of ways to slow down?

What's Essential Will Happen

Sometimes time seems to be running through our hands. We fear we might not have enough time. We are afraid some things which are essential to us might not happen, due to a lack of time.

I have experienced this myself. I tried to force things, fearing them never to happen otherwise. But it doesn't work this way. What if we could learn to accept that what is essential will happen. Anyway! And if things don't seem to happen? Even though we believe they are crucial to us, what could be the reason for this?

Nothing comes without a price. Sometimes we crave something and don't realize that deep inside we are not willing to pay the fee. We want more money, but we despise the effort it would take to get it. We want to be in a relationship, but we don't agree to the necessary compromises relationships tend to include. We want to gain or lose weight, but we are not willing to change our eating habits. We suggest caring more for our environment, but we don't take the necessary steps to change.

Often things have happened to me in my life which I hated and caused me to suffer. It was awful coping with my husband's death, and all the s**t I had to take care of afterwards. Looking back, even though a part of me is still mourning, more pieces of me cherish the changes to my life this sad event made possible. Every lover leaving me, every job proposal rejected, every opportunity missed, in hindsight, they all turned out to be the best things that could happen to me. Even if it sometimes took a while for me to realize this.

You need not force things to happen or try to will things into existence. Use your precious time by valuing everything that takes place, taking advantage of every possibility that opens up to you, cultivating your relationship with every friend you win. Most of all, use every opportunity you get to contribute. Giving, I have experienced, is the best way of winning for yourself.

I'd like to finish with a quote from May Sarton: *"I always forget how important the empty days are, how important it may be sometimes not to expect to produce anything, even a few lines in a journal. A day when one has not pushed oneself to the limit seems a damaged damaging day, a sinful day. Not so! The most valuable thing one can do for the psyche, occasionally, is to let it rest, wander, live in the changing light of a room."*

So, how do you relate to time? And, is it how you WANT it to be?

Dune Plants

Caroline Harvey (Spain)

Today a bed of yellow,
Warm colours on a hot spring day.
Tomorrow the sand garden
Will have shifted.
Another colour,
Different shapes.
Seen through the fresh lens
Of my wandering, wondering mind.

Key to Excellence

Claudia Brose (Germany)

I believe the ability to pay attention, that is to focus, to care and be aware, is a key to excellence, in both our personal and professional lives

How to Avoid Being Ambushed by a Meaningless Life

Jeremy Deedes (UK)

How I came to understand that a world based on compassion and service is infinitely more rewarding than one based on greed and self-interest.

It is July 2014, and I have returned to Lourdes after a break of over forty years. The first time I travelled to this holy shrine in France was in 1972. Now, for the second time in my life, I am part of a group of pilgrims taking over 80 sick and disabled people to Lourdes for a week of spiritual, mental and physical renewal.

This week of service has become deeply significant for me. It is the most essential week in my year, and I have returned to Lourdes once or twice nearly every year since 2014. The disappointment I felt at the pandemic-enforced cancellations of 2020 and 2021 have only reinforced Lourdes' importance for me. It has cemented a fundamental understanding that has grown in me over the years: meaning is found by focussing on others, not by looking inwards.

In Lourdes, for a week in July, compassion takes the number one slot. It is hard work for the volunteers. From five or six in the morning, we are involved in looking after those in our care. And whilst we can take breaks, we don't really come off duty until ten at night, after which there is a need to unwind in one of the local bars – a process that can go on until two or three in the morning.

A conventional career

Lourdes now epitomises the life of meaning I have sought since I was a young adult. However, after my first Lourdes pilgrimage in 1972, I go conventional. I follow a career in the Services, then the City, where a combination of bad choices, bad mistakes and unclear values leads to a meaningless life in which fear and scarcity predominate.

So this is the story of how I came full circle back to a world where compassion takes precedence over egotism and contribution is more important than consumption. I felt I never had enough in my younger days and that I was not enough, hence the greed and fear. Now I know I am enough and have enough. So I tell my story to inspire and encourage those who instinctively feel that they are not in a good place, especially those who know it but don't know where or how to move forward.

In truth, my metamorphosis came about partly through meeting the right people at the right time. However, it also came from making mistakes and learning from them. I now see my mistakes as my greatest asset, even if the world was pear-shaped at the time.

My story begins in the late 1970s when I make an inept error of judgement. As a result, I crash out of the Services in a blaze of bad publicity. Sadly, the references, thanks and support I receive from my superiors and brother officers are not enough to set me back on my feet. I spend the next two decades in the City imitating Chuchundra the Muskrat, a character from The Jungle Book by Rudyard Kipling. Chuchundra is the timid and fearful opposite of Rikki-Tikki-Tavi, the fearless mongoose who takes him under his wing.[1] Like Chuchundra, I fear being seen lest the cobras Nag and Nagaina in the form of the press and other enemies pounce on me.

I have joined the crowds following the money, and I live on a diet of fear, egotism, greed and alcohol. I survive by protecting myself with a skin-deep profile, staying close to the wall and in the shadows.

So I remember well the sheer horror at addressing an audience of over two hundred City captains at a fund launch. Some of this fear comes, of course, from the physical act of standing up and speaking. However, I am also petrified at being found out. I realise now that this fear also comes from the risk to my integrity. My meaningless life has the potential to ambush me.

The lack of faith in myself and my work back then contrasts sharply to the ease with which I can speak or write about the things that matter to me now.

But, looking back, I realise that the biggest mistake in my life is not dealing with my earliest mistakes. I only learn to do this properly much later from Brené Brown[1], who encourages us to write our story free from the confabulations and lies we used to shield ourselves from the pain and shame of our mistakes. It takes countless iterations, starting with the advice from author Anne Lamott to write a *"shitty first draft"*[23]. But, over time, the truth overtakes the lies, and I learn about myself from my mistakes.

Living with scarcity and unhappiness

Back in the City, I am not happy, and if I refuse to admit this to myself, it is clearly evident to others. Even my parents tell me to my face and ask me why I don't leave my job. The answer, of course, is that I am living a life of scarcity, or so I think. I do not have enough money, prestige, self-worth, meaning or company, and I feel the only place I will find enough is in the City.

Because I have not fully resolved or learnt the lessons of my first mistake, I make the next big mistake in my life. Egged on by the scarcity I feel and the siren songs of fabulous wealth and great careers that come to MBAs, I borrow money, take a year out and study for an MBA.

As I finish my MBA, the 90/91 recession hits, and I cannot get a job. My finances deteriorate. I hit a low point. I feel like a fraud and a failure because I am supposed to be an expert with money, and now I have no income, no assets and significant debts. I am worthless, ashamed and humiliated, so much so that I cut ties with my family and friends, which only makes things worse.

However, this precipitates, at last, a seismic shift in my thinking, giving rise to the powerful insights that shape my future career. I don't want to get control of money, which has been my main driving force to date, but I realise I have to get control of my life. I start to recognise that money is a means to an end, not an end in itself. To think only about making more money misses the point of money.

At last, I am beginning to learn some of life's most important lessons, not least that facing up to my mistakes is far better than running from them, even if it's painful at the time. However, I am still in thrall to the power of money, which has such a constricting effect on my life, but I realise that something has to change. It's just that I don't know where to go or how to change.

A turning point

So it is fortunate that in July 2004, I meet George Kinder, the father of life planning. He takes me on a journey that changes everything and brings me back to a contented, compassionate life, focused on others, not myself, and which revolves around contributing more than I consume.

The meeting was no coincidence, even though it came just at the right time for me. We meet at Kinder's signature **Seven Stages of Money Maturity** workshop, the first to be held in the UK. By then, I have built a good network of contacts, one of whom mentions the event. In fact, he does more than mention it. He overcomes my cynicism and sells it to me even though I remain sceptical of this American who preaches such alien concepts as empathy, listening and compassion[4].

Kinder is the kick I need, however. I spend the next ten years or so in his company, off and on. And it is not just Kinder. The community of people I meet in this new arena are the antithesis of my earlier values. They teach me the power of compassion and care. They are supportive and non-judgmental listeners. They encourage me to be vulnerable and help me come to emotional terms with my experience in the Services.

They encourage me to work with a therapist. This helps me regain my confidence, find my purpose in life and discover a new world where you is far more significant than me.

I build my own financial life planning business, **Planning for Life**, on the back of this newfound confidence and my revised values. It is slow and steady progress as I create a long-term client base founded on trust, service and a defined charging structure incorporating full fee transparency.

I relinquished my authorisation to provide financial advice in 2016. Thirty years of rules and regulations are more than enough. I hand over my clients to a fellow financial planner I know I can trust. As I leave the industry, the financial rewards that accrue to me are far greater than anticipated. I accept them with grace as the returns from building a long-term business defined by the lessons learnt from my earlier mistakes. This is the value of trust and putting my clients ahead of their money.

Completing the circle

And now I am beginning to recycle that wealth for the benefit of others. I used a small amount to get formal coaching training and a postgraduate certificate. More of it is being used to develop my new **Crazy for Change** programme, designed to help people achieve meaning in their lives by helping others find meaning in theirs. As Lynn Twist, author of **The Soul of Money**, succinctly points out, wealth is like water[4]. It stagnates if it remains in a pond, whilst wealth that flows like water creates change and makes a difference in the world.

Now I wake up in the morning with the knowledge that I have mastered my own life and money. I can look at myself in the mirror and face the world. I am happy and have found meaning and purpose in helping others deal with similar problems to my own. I now understand that a world based on compassion and service is infinitely more rewarding than one based on greed. In short, I have enough and I am enough. I have gained emotional and financial maturity and am, at last, in a good place.

References

(1) Brown, B (2015).Rising Strong. Vermillion, London

(2) Lamott, A (1994).Bird by Bird: Some Instructions On Writing and Life. Pantheon, New York

(3) See https://www.kinderinstitute.com

(4) Twist, L (2003).The Soul of Money. WW Norton, New York

Always Enough ...

Ulla Raaf (Germany)

Empathy

Naturalness

Optimism

Understanding

Generosity

Honesty

About Claudia Brose

Claudia is a quiet trailblazer who always looks off the beaten path for new ideas and inspirations about how we can combine our personal life and work life in a fulfilling way.

Her international experience in both business and Asian culture and philosophy has led her to her current work in raising awareness about the importance of the human element in business. Drawing upon her MBA, international marketing management and nonprofit leadership work in Germany and fourteen years in San Francisco, California, she is now committed to challenging our current mindset about the worlds of conscious living and business.

Through writing, speaking and events she encourages leaders, entrepreneurs and changemakers to advance a new vision of how we can work and live in a wholesome way. In addition, Claudia has built a business that creates memorable events for photography enthusiasts, connecting passionate participants with top professional photographers who lead with their hearts. She has initiated a growing community of imaginative creative people.

She considers herself an undeniable optimist, is crazy about everything Japanese, is obsessed with the outdoors and loves travelling the world.

Meet Claudia at:
https://www.claudiabrose.com/
https://www.linkedin.com/in/claudiabrose/
https://www.instagram.com/claudiabrose/

How to Give your Work and Life the Attention they Deserve

Claudia Brose (Germany)

How cultivating an attentive approach to life leads to a humane, respectful and kind approach that makes you a better version of yourself and a better leader, friend, and partner.

"The past twenty years, where did they go?! I don't remember much of it. I went to work, back home, and back to work. That's it!" says a close friend of mine. *"Did you witness your kids growing up?"* I ask. *"Maybe, not really. Sometimes at the dinner table the kids share stories…'remember how we did this and that?' and I can't recall those moments. This made me realize that I missed out on shared experiences with them while they grew up."*

There are many stories like this one. They always leave me puzzled and upset. Why do we tend to pay a lot of attention to work as opposed to our private life and needs? At the same time, we complain about not having enough time for the life we want to live. I wanted to take a different path and my question was: Can we make life less about work and rather make work part of our lifestyle?

I love to work. But I also believe our work life, occupying a third of our day, should be a joyful part of our life, giving us a sense of fulfillment at the end of the day.

What is my version of a happy work and life combination? When I can have control over my time and space, when my work has a purpose and an impact, and when I give enough time to my family, friends, and myself. What is your vision of combining your personal life and work life, so you are happy at the end of the day?

What if we start looking at the lifestyle we want and then create our work life accordingly instead of the other way around?

Self-awareness is key

Living and working in Japan for a while after finishing university in Germany was fascinating because I love experiencing life and work from a completely different perspective. For some reason, I always had and still have a thing for Asia. I returned to my home country Germany, and after seven years of building a career in the marketing world, an inner voice kept coming up. A voice telling me to move again into the world. I paid attention to my inner voice, I listened. I moved to San Francisco, helping a friend build a business around Asian artifacts and interiors.

What did I pay attention to and why?

There was this feeling of dissatisfaction with my work because I lost seeing the purpose in it and I got itchy to work and live in an international environment. While building a career I became aware of several characteristics my work needs to offer for me to feel motivated, stimulated, and satisfied with my work life.

Temporal and spatial flexibility and freedom, diversity in the work projects, intellectual challenges, and international exchange are important for me. I couldn't check all these boxes anymore. So I quit and packed up.

How much attention do you pay to your work and career and how much to the other aspects of life? Work seems very often to overshadow everything else.

Self-awareness is key. Understanding your purpose, principles and values are the first steps that serve to guide you when deciding who or what you want to spend your time on amid the overwhelming demands and distractions of daily life.

The interconnectedness of different life areas

Several major areas of life need our attention when it comes to living in a fulfilling and satisfying way. Health and Body, Work and Career (finances, education, achievements), Family and Social Life (friends, maintaining relationships, meeting new people), Personal Development (intellectual, spiritual, creative inspirations), Life Vision and Quality of Life.

This is about evaluating and balancing each part of your life and becoming aware of the fact that all areas are interconnected and contribute to your overall well-being, personally and professionally. If I get enough sleep, exercise, and time in nature, I am energized, motivated and productive at work. If I am fulfilled at work, I carry my good mood and satisfaction into my private life and am a better spouse, friend, and citizen.

What are your values and visions?

Living ten thousand kilometers away in San Francisco didn't keep me from going back home to Germany regularly to see my family and friends, who I always stay in close touch with no matter where I live. Nurturing friendships and caring for relationships has a high value in my life. This requires a work life that allows me to travel whenever I want or need to and to be able continue working while traveling.

What values do you appreciate and are important to you?

Fourteen years in San Francisco I watched friends and people around me being unhappy in spite of being immersed in successful careers. I noticed that I felt happy even though I left my career path and started something new. It made me question people's perception of themselves and their working life. I was impressed with their tough business appearance but at the same time stunned at how they could be so insecure in their private life.

Do we have to change our authentic selves between working and living? I am happily the same person in private as I am in the working world.

Keep an eye on yourself, perceive what is going on inside you, don't be indifferent to yourself. Start being interested in yourself, take care of the self inside of you, nourish it. What sparks you and what motivates you? Where do you refuse to accept any compromises anymore? What do you not want to miss? Can you tell if you are your authentic self in your daily life and work?

Living and working with attention

While still living in California I continued my vision of connecting business with people, culture and life through different work projects. A couple of years before leaving the country I, together with a business friend in Germany, created an annual photography event in a beautiful location in Northern Italy. Thanks to today's world of automation, digitization, and interconnectedness I could organize everything from across the Atlantic. Eventually, my American husband and I moved to

Europe, for many reasons related to our ideas of where and how we want to work and live.

Imagine you have a treasure inside of you that can help you create your best life and work combination! This treasure is called paying attention.

Why attention and what is it?

I believe the quality of your attention determines the quality of your life. How we experience the world depends crucially on how we deal with our attention. Today's scarcest resource and the secret to high performance and fulfillment is attention. It is an important asset that we too easily waste instead of treasuring.

Paying attention encompasses three essential skills, which makes it so valuable:

- The art of being able to focus your attention
- The willingness to pay sufficient attention to yourself, your loved ones, and the people you work with
- The ability to be aware of your surroundings.

When you can focus your attention on what is the most important you will be able to finish your task or reach your goal much faster. The increase in productivity and learning when we stop trying to do it all at once is astonishing. You waste less time and gain more time for other areas of your life.

Paying sufficient attention to yourself means you care for your mental and physical well-being, reflect your visions and listen to your thoughts. It prevents you from burnout, negative stress, and dissatisfaction. Instead, you gain energy, motivation, and inspiration.

When you give attention to your loved ones and the people you work with you are mindful, thoughtful, considerate, and kind. Appreciating and caring for people takes time. The result is better services and products for your customers, long-lasting relationships with loved ones, and motivated, productive, and loyal employees and colleagues.

Applying attention to daily life and work means adopting an attitude of selection, awareness, and kindness. When you choose to pay attention you are actually paying with something valuable.

The value of attention

The photography event is a growing community of enthusiastic people who love coming back because they feel taken care of and enjoy a unique atmosphere of respect, support, and appreciation. We pay attention to them. Paul, a business owner and passionate amateur photographer who participates regularly tells me: "*What I love about this event is that it feels very authentic and honest. You really want to help us to become better and the workshop leaders share so generously their knowledge and experience*". The participants reward us with their regular return, enthusiastic participation, and connection throughout the year.

Paying attention is an effort. To be polite, to listen, to focus is hard work. To be thoughtful, considerate, mindful, and caring requires time and consciousness. Taking time to reflect, to go deeper, to deal with yourself, and to notice what is happening around you is not easy and requires a constant state of awareness and openness.

This is exhausting and it takes a lot of self-discipline. But it's worth the effort. Because the ability to pay attention is a key to excellence, in both our personal and professional lives.

Enough – Is there a limit to how much attention we can give?

Your potential to give attention is limited. We can only pay so much attention to several things or tasks or voices or stimulations in a certain time frame. But it is up to us to decide what we pay attention to or if we let our boss, our work demands, or media and marketing platforms take over and steal your attention from us.

The glass half-filled with water is what it is. It is halfway filled. Now it is up to you how you look at the glass. If you look at it as half full you are thinking in terms of abundance. If you look at it as half empty you have a mindset of scarcity. Who gives, receives. When we give attention, we get attentive behavior back.

This is a mindset of abundance. If we pay attention to our customers or audience and try to understand their desires and problems, then they will put us in the spotlight. If we listen to our employees, acknowledge and respect them, they will reward us with their commitment, ideas, and loyalty. When we pay attention to our loved ones we receive support, joy, and love. Attention is abundant.

To be attentive means that you are on a constant quest to be aware, awake and alert. How to combine work and life is a question of lifestyle. Thinking about how you want to combine life and work is about defining what lifestyle you want to create.

Paying attention is a mindset, a way of being. It's a lifestyle. It's a basic philosophy for living. What you give your attention to is your choice. And it is your choice to deny those who want to grab your attention at their convenience.

Is life absorbing you or do you absorb life? Cultivating an attentive approach to life results in a humane, respectful and kind approach to yourself, others and the workplace. It results in becoming a better version of yourself, a better leader, friend and partner. As Jim Rohn says: "*Give whatever you are doing and whoever you are with the gift of your attention.*"

Calling

Kim LeClair (USA)

between buzzing and binging and beeping
live
small
moments
watching a dog sleep
witnessing a tree bend in the breeze
wiping chocolate from a child's face
wake up to the wonder
wedged amid
chatter and clutter and clatter
calling you
nudging you
to notice

About Cat Preston

Cat Preston is an iPEC certified life coach helping people discover their core strengths and talents so that they can do work they love and be the change they seek to make in the world.

She also works as a coach for both Seth Godin's altMBA, an intensive online leadership programme for people who want to do work that matters, and The StorySkills Workshop, which helps people tell better stories that engage, influence and inspire others.

Cat's colourful travels over the past twenty years, calling six different countries on three continents home, teaching, and running a jewellery business have borne witness to the social and environmental challenges our world is facing, in high definition. Seeing the world through that multicultural lens has taught her to question narratives and embrace curiosity.

Sharing what she has learnt along the way to help and encourage others who want to turn their dreams into sustainable, heart-centred, purpose-driven businesses, is work that inspires her.

Cat is also the host of The Collective Wisdom podcast sharing the stories of connection, creativity, kindness and challenges from her guests and getting to the heart of what it means to be human.

When she's not working, you'll find her out in nature hiking, biking or growing wildflowers.

She currently lives with her husband, three children, a dog, a cat and a colony of bees in rural Gloucestershire in the UK.

Meet Cat at:
www.catpreston.com
www.linkedin.com/in/cat-preston-b977353b
https://www.instagram.com/collectivewisdom_pod/

Collective Wisdom – The Highs and Lows of Launching a Podcast

Cat Preston (UK)

"Everyone you will ever meet knows something you don't." Bill Nye

This is the story of The Collective Wisdom Podcast. How it came into being and why it's so important to follow your creative dreams.

My Uncle William died recently. He was only 71. He was not only a lovely man but also a very talented surgeon. He embraced life and when he wasn't working, he loved to ski or cycle in the mountains, or take to the air – he got his pilot's licence shortly after his 60th Birthday. Tragically, at the age of 62, shortly after he retired, he was diagnosed with Alzheimer's disease and spent the last two years of his life in a nursing home.

The last time I spoke to him he had almost lost his language skills and was easily confused, but we were sitting having a simple supper in his kitchen the night before his third grandchild was going to be christened. I asked him how it felt to have saved so many lives throughout his career and his face lit up in a smile. He visibly rose in his seat and picked up the table knife in front of him and started to demonstrate. *"You put the thing in the thing and then join it up. Sometimes. Simple really."* *"Simple for you maybe, but I can't imagine even getting close to cutting someone open,"* I laughed.

In that moment of pure lucidity, he was clearly back in the operating theatre skilfully cutting and snipping and stitching. Doing what he had done so many times that it came naturally to him. It's how I want to remember him. In his element and smiling. Knowing how much we thought of him and the positive impact he'd made on the lives of so many others.

I think it was that conversation and the many others I'd had when I was working in my first job as a nursing auxiliary in a care home for the elderly that taught me how it is so much easier to connect with others if you strive to be the most interested person in the room rather than the most interesting.

Ask any one of those elderly residents about a photograph on the windowsill or a locket around their neck and there was always a story there. Taking time to stop being busy making beds or serving tea to sit down and listen whilst they revisited happy memories was the kindest thing you could ever do for them.

So when the pandemic hit and we were all forced to take a collective pause and given the opportunity to step out of the busyness of our everyday lives and reflect on what really matters, I realised that for me there were two things.

Firstly, relationships.

I knew I valued those connections with family and friends above all else. Not being able to see loved ones for a prolonged period brought it home to me. Had I been taking it for granted that they would always be there? When was the last time I'd actually told any of them how much I really loved or appreciated them?

And then, making the most of my time here.

Seeing heart-breaking footage of lives cut short, hearing stories of the huge holes left in people's lives by the loss of loved ones, and knowing that my Uncle William could never have predicted how his final years would play out, made me pause and think about some of the things I'd regret never having done if life were cut short.

What was at the top of my dream list? To host a podcast. Podcasts have been such a source of inspiration and learning for me.

Discovering **The High Low** with Dolly Alderton and Pandora Sykes back in 2017 just as I'd moved back to the UK after 20 years of living overseas to a small village where I knew nobody had been such a godsend. They were wise, creative and kind, as well as being killingly funny at times. Bringing them along for company as I walked the dog was pure joy. I can still remember exactly where I was standing the day they announced that after four years they would be bringing the party to an end as they had other dreams they needed to pursue. Like the sadness of a farewell when a friend leaves for a new country, knowing they will always be there but the close bond between you will inevitably fade with time.

Or my other firm favourite which happily is still going, **How to Fail** with Elizabeth Day. It's like a mini therapy session each week. Sharing stories about the things that haven't gone right, connecting, and creating a deeper understanding of how we process failure.

So that's what I wanted to craft and create. Elizabeth Day meets Dolly and Pandora.

The real challenge was where to start. And how to get through the messy part of not being perfect or even a tenth of what I wanted it to be straight out of the gate. I signed up for Akimbo's podcasting fellowship. They helped me to break it down into bite-sized chunks.

What would my podcast be called? Who would it be for? How would I find them? I fought with my technical phobia and little by little learnt how to use Audacity to record. As is often the case, it was way easier than I thought once I got used to it.

I overcame the uncomfortable, toe-curlingly cringemaking aversion to hearing those first recordings of my voice being played back to me. Worse than that was the voice in my head that told me I was mad. Why was I doing this?

I recorded the first intro and played it to my kids to a mixed response:

"*Can you turn it off, it's triggering me,*" from Josh.

Slightly gentler, but equally damning, "*It's a good message, but it doesn't really sound like you, Mum,*" from Jake.

"*Mmm. It sounds more like you're one of those women in a spa who is trying to get everyone to relax,*" from Hana.

They clearly wanted to let me down gently (or not so gently in Josh's case) and protect me from the seemingly inevitable public humiliation that was bound to follow if they didn't intervene and nip this nonsense in the bud. I loved them for their honesty and the urge to save me from myself.

Every bit of me wanted to agree. To stop and hang up my podcasting boots even though I hadn't got to the first post. It all felt so far from my dream.

And then something magical happened. I got on a call with a fellow coach friend of mine called Nick. He asked me how things were going, and I told him about the podcast and my hopes and aspirations for it. "*It's about sharing stories and the fact we can learn something from everyone if we just take the time to listen,*" I said.

Without even knowing where it came from, I explained that I'd come to see the power of stories to connect and build trust. So, I'd be asking my guests to share three stories. An act of simple kindness that's impacted them, because kindness is such an undervalued currency. A challenge they've overcome and what they learnt from it, because I want everyone to see just how much strength and courage and enoughness they have inside them. And a piece of music that means something to them, because I'm such a fan of Desert Island Discs and the stories it elicits with that simple question. Music is such a universal language we can all relate to.

Then I'd get everyone to share one piece of wisdom that has helped them because nobody knows everything but together we know a lot. I was getting into my stride now. All the fear of not being good enough to actually deliver this had left me for a moment as I engaged with why it mattered.

"Sounds amazing, Cat," Nick replied. *"I'd love to take part if you'd have me. We could record it next week."*

I think it was in that moment, as my stomach lurched and I could sense nausea rising, that I realised I was never going to feel ready or confident enough to do this. I was just going to have to make a very fearful start and hope that I could channel my inner Elizabeth Day when I needed to.

Nick then sent me his stories and I couldn't have wished for a more resounding and emphatic nudge from the universe that I was on the right path. His act of simple kindness and the challenge were related as his mother had died of cancer when he was 13. The kindest thing she could have done for him after she found out it was terminal was to sit down and talk him through what he could expect at her funeral. He couldn't imagine doing the same for one of his own children, but said it had helped him enormously when the day came.

He shared that the challenge for him had been losing her at the time, but also understanding how to grieve by keeping her memory alive. Talking about her on his wedding day was harder in many ways than losing her when he was younger.

And then he told a beautiful story about the song **American Pie** by Don Mclean. It had been the music he and his sisters and dad had listened to on holidays in Cornwall both before his mother died and after she'd had to leave. It was an obvious choice as the song to play as their first dance at his wedding.

Here he was confirming that we all have a story and just how much these stories matter. They are where we find the truth and wisdom to understand each other and ourselves better.

It took four more months of agonising and waiting to feel ready, between making that first recording and actually pressing go on this project.

I got myself a producer so that I couldn't let myself off the hook. Chris is kind and patient. He seemed to sense that when I didn't deliver on time it wasn't laziness or lack of respect for the timelines we had put in place. It was fear. I finally launched two weeks before Christmas. And when I say launch, there was no fanfare or grand announcement. I needed to let it just quietly be out there.

I'm now thirty episodes in. I've been able to capture these precious stories from family, friends, mentors and people I admire. I get to reach out to them and tell them that they are the sort of kind, wise people from whom we need to hear more. I'm so grateful to them all for their openness and for trusting me with their incredible stories.

I'm happy to say that podcasting has become far easier with time and practice. Like Uncle William in the operating theatre, I'm finding that with competence comes confidence.

It's been met with such kind words of encouragement and support (even Josh has given it a nod of approval), all of which has made my heart feel full. I feel closer and more connected to guests and listeners alike. I even had the pleasure of meeting Elizabeth in person to tell her what an inspiration she's been to me.

But the best feeling of all is knowing that I have pushed through that limiting fear to the other side. As a coach, I partner with people all the time, coaxing them to work through the fear of stepping into the unknown, or to question the belief that they're not good enough. It feels so good to be right there at the sharp end with them.

So, what is your wildest dream? That small flame of an idea that won't leave you be? What I've come to know is that if you're able to dream it, you have what it takes inside you to turn that dream into a reality.

You are more than enough.

For What it's Worth: A Love Letter to my Children

Cat Preston (UK)

Hey my loves,

For what it's worth, here's a few things my friends have taught me along the way.

Life really is about the journey, not the destination. Each new day as the sun rises, there's a gift to begin again. Kindness is the currency that connects us all. Spend it freely, especially on yourself. Communication is kind, even the truths that are hard to say. Understand that nothing lasts, even the good stuff, so live every day that way. Trust that the only person you can ever really compare yourself to is who you were yesterday. So, if you're doing your best, it's always good enough.

For what it's worth, there will be challenges along the way. But there are also many solutions. Start by looking inward at yourself with compassion and kindness. When you find it in yourself, you'll see it in others.

And when there's a bump in the road, walk through it not around it. It always seems impossible until it's done. You'll find your place in the world when you can live in integrity with yourself. Honour who you truly are, and just resolve to shine.

For what it's worth, the opposite of love isn't hate, it's fear. Often the best answer is just to listen. Especially to the people who love you. It takes humility to know your own limits and find the courage to ask for help or to know when to let go. Remind yourself in times of darkness that This too is for the best. And that every wound will teach you resilience and courage. Remember to breathe, slow down, and look back at how far you've come. Then be brave and take the next step without knowing where it will take you.

For what it's worth, don't stress the could haves – if it should have been, it would have been. Know that inside every regret, there's a lesson. Learn from your past to build your future and never stop growing. And always remember, a little bit of gratitude goes a long, long way. I'm so grateful to you three for the joy you've afforded your dad and me. You taught us to stay connected to child within us and to dance in puddles in the rain.

For what you're worth, is immeasurable. As dusk falls and the moon comes out each night, look up with a smile and know just how much are loved.

All my love, always,
Mum xoxo

Creativity Tops Money

Ulla Raaf (Germany)

Nothing is more unnecessary than investing in customers who don't understand, care for, want, or need you.

Marketing is communication. Or, as Bernadette Jiwa once said: *"Marketing is helpful conversations."* Often, we tend to think we must have a huge budget to work out our marketing. There are tons of ways to get in contact with your people. Ads, blogs, books, trade fairs, the internet, social media, podcasts, open houses, tutorials, webinars, key-note-speaking, to name but a few. If we think more about what we are trying to achieve instead of how, we gain focus.

Concentrate on the more important question: Why? Whatever you are planning, keep asking yourself, why in all heavens somebody should choose you. Why should they notice you, become interested in you, decide for you and, pay for you? Change your messages from what you have to offer to why you do so. Tell your prospects or customers why you do things, how you do so and why that counts.

It would be best if you got these questions very clear at the beginning. Only then can you start thinking about how to communicate this. I have experienced that creativity tops money. Or in other terms: You don't need a big budget – something often scarce to small companies or start-ups – but you do need creative ideas.

Remember, marketing is a combination of advertising, promotion, publicity, public relations and sales. Not only do I want to encourage you to think differently about your approach to your marketing, but I also want to give you input on how to do so. In the following passages, I share some ideas I have gathered.

Excitement

Some years ago in Mainz, the city I live in, you could find postcards randomly distributed in different pubs and shops. They said nothing else but: *"Etwas Dickes kommt in die Stadt"*, which means *"Something Fat is Coming into the City."* Even on Facebook, similar posts would pop up now and then. It happened for several weeks. Then all of a sudden there was an address added. In a corner house in a picturesque part of Mainz, the cafe Dicke Lilli, gutes Kind was opened. It translates to Fat Lilli, Good Child, which is the title of the bestselling book by Lilli Palmer, a famous actress in Germany, known for her love of cake too.

In the cafe, you will find several utterly different-looking dining tables and chairs and fantastic wall decorations. Different antique place settings containing a plate, saucer, and cup are glued on top of each other and then symmetrically fixed to one wall. The cafe provides fresh homebaked cakes and a daily changing lunch. It has always been very well frequented ever since.

Excitement is the number one motivational method in literature. Whether love stories, thrillers, life stories, or fantasy, you keep reading because you want to know what comes next, how it will end, or what the result will be.

How can you make your offering exciting? Can the interaction with your prospects be exciting? What if, like this café, you built up and guided your customers through to a crescendo?

Attention

Today Paula visits a cafe wanting to relax and surround herself with people. After tasting it, she delightedly reports to the server that their redcurrant meringue cake is exceptional. What an enjoyable afternoon.

Several weeks later, she has errands to do and some time leftover. Fortunately, she happens to be near the little cafe and decides to go there. The server coming to take her order mentions that today there is redcurrant meringue cake, too, if she would like some. Paula is impressed that he remembers.

People love it when we remember things about them and mention them sometime later. Try to gain as much information about your contacts as possible. There cannot be too much. If people remember the details we told them, we feel important and valued. In this regard, your customers are people, too. The more you know about them, the better you can use this to serve them and your relationship.

Curiosity

A while ago I was contracted by a company to do the concept and design for a conventional mailing via letters. Due to costs, the only viable format was a standard letter, in this case with a window envelope. Instead of using the envelope as usually done, I decided to design the letter so that there would only be an over-dimensioned eye visible in the window, looking at the recipient. He should desperately want to know what this is about.

People have an innate curiosity. Just imagine little children, touching, examining and trying everything out. If you can pique one's interest, you can be sure to stand out and get attention.

How could you make your target market curious? How could you satisfy existing curiosity? Why not go and play with the curiousness of your customer?

Gathering Instincts

A consultant put small tips about her topic together to a pretty designed quartet play. She sent these cards to a specifically handpicked bunch of target people one at a time together with an interestingly composed letter containing some advice related to the card. When she finished the mailing series, the recipients were surprised with an appropriate box for the cards, too.

She created something of value that probably nobody will throw away and will remind her customers from time to time about her services. What would prick the gathering instincts of your customers?

Play Instincts

I remember my excitement with my first Apple Macintosh quite well. Even deleting a file was something completely new and unique: you dragged the file over the trash bin, dropped it there, and you could even see the trash bin expanding. When pressing the delete button, a funny hiss proved the deletion had taken place. I truly believe that Apple's tremendous success not only relies on its ground-breaking ability to keep things simple and logical via its exceptional design but also on serving the instinct to play.

How could you serve the play instincts of your customers? What could you offer that combines both playfulness and usefulness?

Emotions

I remember watching a very emotional video about a blind beggar sitting on the street-side on a beautiful sunny day. In front of him, besides his hat to collect alms, a sign reads: I'm blind. The video shows the whole thing from the beggar's perspective, so you can only see passerbys' legs and shoes. Quite rarely, somebody throws a coin into the hat.

Then a woman passes, recognizable as such through her silk stockings and red heels. She stops, picks up the sign, and you can hear her writing something but can't read it. Afterwards you notice that, nearly every passerby throws a coin into the hat. She wrote: "*It's a beautiful day and I can't see it.*" Every time I tell this story, I break into tears.

If someone addresses our compassion, we tend to be much more cooperative if we are touched by what we are experiencing. How could you speak to your customers emotionally? How could you arrange your offer, so it targets the emotional side of your customers? What would make them cry, laugh, fear, hope?

Empathy

Tanja has been working for her customer Ellie for years. What used to be a working relationship had become a friendship. At a particular birthday party, Ellie invites everyone important to her on her life's way. She chooses Tanja as one of them.

The party includes the presentation of all guests. Most of them don't know each other. Ellie introduces Tanja in the following way: „*I know Tanja from working together with her. We have done quite some projects together so far. I can tell you in summary what I love about working with her. Tanja listens very carefully and therefore can empathize with her customers so well that her suggestions are of a kind you could never have come up with, never would have imagined. Yet they are exactly what you want.*"

How could you empathize with your customers' dreams, wishes, and imaginations, so they would love to do work with you? How would you show prospects that you exactly understand what they need and provide a practical solution?

Surprise

This one I read in Bernadette Jiwa's Blog, The Story of Telling: On a busy street in a middle size town, the tenth hairdresser opens his shop. It happens to be one of those who offer $10 haircuts. Fearing competition and losing customers, all of the other hairdressers slowly comply and become $10 hairdressers too. All, except for one. She puts a sign in her window reading: „*I fix $10 haircuts.*"

We love to be surprised. Think about birthday presents, about telephone calls you didn't expect, a sudden miraculous change for the better in a precarious situation, or the surprising end of a story.

How can you surprise your customer? How can you surprisingly communicate your offer? Which unexpected stylistic elements like colors, pictures, stories, or arrangements can you use?

Story-Telling

Everybody loves stories. Stories affect. They fascinate, delight, teach, empathize, and are enjoyable. We identify with the protagonists, we suffer, love, laugh, and live with them.

Simon Sinek says: *„People don't buy what you offer, but why you offer this!"* Let your customers participate with your visions, inspirations, and struggles so they can identify themselves with those.

Stories have a clear structure with a beginning, middle, and end. Think about which theme you could write. Plan a clear concept around which the story evolves. You can divide it into several chapters. Of course, your story needs a hero as well as a villain, which can be a problem, challenge, struggle, or obstacle to overcome. Describe different phases the hero experiences on a path to the climax of the story and the decisive change marking the point where the hero manages the challenge.

Use story-telling whenever possible. It makes everything much more interesting and captivating than a simple description. Let the story provide information about what your customer could achieve when choosing your offer. You will reach many more people when choosing an emotional story over a rational instruction. People make sales decisions by the heart rather than the brain. To enable the customer to see the offer's effect, make sure you address all senses like seeing, hearing, feeling, smelling, or tasting. Promise to fulfill needs like joy, happiness, relief, help, usefulness. Use this compelling way to convince anyone, making it very clear what someone can expect in this respect. Stories are an excellent way to help people share aspects of your offer. If you show how you are different, people will recognize why this counts.

How to continue

You may have found some inspiration in this essay. The dominating obstacles in marketing, especially for small enterprises or start-ups, can be having plans that are too big and not enough resources. Be careful when it comes to your time or capacities. I prefer small viable steps over too many or too big plans. It would help if you didn't necessarily do it all alone. Think about how you could involve external help.

Your customer should remain central to all activities. The more you know about his needs, the better you can serve. Don't suspect what your customer might want. Provide strategies for how to find out what matters to him.

Think about what you would like for yourself. Use this in your interactions with your customers. First, you will like it because it will feel natural to you, and second, you will be on the same wavelength as your customer. Nothing is more unnecessary than investing in customers who don't understand, care for, want, or need you. If there is no fit, work, even if it should come, won't be easy. Misunderstandings will happen more often, and it will drain your energy.

Work per definition serves two main goals: to serve your customers and to serve yourself as well. If you see to that, comfortable and sustainable relationships will come about. And always remember: it is much easier to cultivate existing customer relationships than to create new ones.

A Fresh Start

Cat Preston (UK)

May I wake
ready for that daily, yet
greatest of gifts;

a fresh start

MORNING AFFIRMATION

To Keep Going

Kim LeClair (USA)

to keep going when the trip gets tough
to keep walking when the way gets rough

if you want the prize much longed for
you have to press on, be strong more

you knew it would not be easy
that the hills might make you queasy

you set out, a dream in your heart
you have to keep going, through this hard part

as you strive and stride
let purpose be your guide

remember for what you aspire
that is the fuel for your fire

Time For a Bit of a Think

Jeremy Deedes (UK)

"Get a cup of tea, sit down and have a bit of a think."
Jodi Taylor

When I set up Planning for Life, a financial life planning consultancy, in 1996, I didn't know what I was doing. Eventually, I learnt how important it was to step back and think about how the business could provide me, my clients and my team with enough of what we wanted. Later, I compiled all these thought processes into a comprehensive business blueprint, an essential tool for creating a business that would meet my definition of successful.

I knew what I wanted Planning for Life to provide: control of my life, happiness and fun, a return to my rural roots, a decent and secure income. And, most importantly, in the deeper parts of myself, I was longing for meaning. So in 1996, I wanted to build a business that would bring meaning into my life by making a difference to others.

In all these, I was successful – in the end. However, it was slow and steady progress. Arguably, this was for several reasons, not least because my values, aspirations and priorities were changing as my interest swung towards my clients as individuals and away from their money. I realised that if I wanted to lead a life that was enough for me and help my clients do the same, I had to stop running and start thinking.

As I did, I found myself drawn more towards the coaching and support that my clients wanted. Yes, financial product advice was necessary, but the real value came from helping clients develop and achieve their goals. So, dealing with their money became a process of structuring clients' finances to support their aspirations.

I also began to realise the value of ongoing professional development. However, every time I learnt a new and exciting way of running a business, I would implement it in Planning for Life, leaving it looking like a dog's breakfast rather than a professional, coherent and structured business.

It was a bit of a dog's breakfast

For instance, I recall a consultant coming up with the idea of creating different services for different markets and writing a set of service standards for each. His advice would have worked, except I designed the services around a poorly defined set of audiences that differentiated each service by my offering rather than the market need. As a result, both I and my prospects were left confused.

At one point, I went into partnership with another planner. Unfortunately, it did not last long. One of the reasons was that neither of us had a clear idea of what we wanted the business to look like – or if we did, we never spent any time reconciling our ideas and developing a shared vision.

And this, I think, was the heart of the dog's breakfast. I did not have a clear vision of what Planning for Life should look like or where it should be.

Instead, it reminded me of the conversation between Alice and the Cheshire Cat[1]. Alice: "*Would you tell me, please, which way I ought to go from here?*" The Cheshire Cat: "*That depends a good deal on where you want to get to.*" Alice: "*I don't much care where …*" The Cheshire Cat: "*Then it doesn't matter which way you go.*" Alice: "*… so long as I get SOMEWHERE.*" The Cheshire Cat: "*Oh, you're sure to do that, if you only walk long enough.*"

Given how many changes I made, I remain surprised at how my clients stuck with me. They were long-suffering and understanding, for which I am grateful.

Stop doing and instead, have a bit of a think

I still hear the enthusiasm of new entrepreneurs mixed with frustration that it's not working. I found the answer to this puzzle brilliantly articulated by Dr Madeline Maxwell, head of the fictional History Department at St Mary's Institute of Historical Research. St Mary's, created by author Jodi Taylor, is where Dr Maxwell leads a team of time travellers. Sorry, I mean leads a team who investigate major historical events in contemporary time. They are also disaster magnets who often find themselves in deep trouble. But, with all her experience, Dr Maxwell has learnt not to panic or do the first thing that comes into her head. Instead, she *"makes a cup of tea, sits down and has a bit of a think."*[2]

Even before I read Taylor, I had begun to apply the mantra, and it worked well for me in one key aspect of my Planning for Life business. I realised it is difficult for anyone to come in cold and buy your main product for what could be a significant amount of money. So instead, I sought some help, had a bit of a think with pen and paper, and designed and built a set of product steps for clients. The bottom step was simply a set of free material, blog posts, articles etc., to allow prospects to find out about us and how we worked.

My next step involved productising my initial discovery meeting. At the time, financial planners usually provided a free, unstructured interview, so I gave it some thought and turned mine into a structured product with three price/service levels. Next, I gave it a name (The Planning for Life Mapmaker) and a tag line (plan your route to integrity and freedom). Finally, I designed a structure and delivery process to end with a sales conversation around my main product. Amazingly, it worked. Although I got slightly fewer meetings, my conversion rate rose significantly.

At the same time, I thought long and hard about my commission-based charging structure and changed it to a simple, clear and transparent fee structure. Surprisingly, I had no difficulty in transferring existing clients onto the new fee format. Indeed, they found the certainty reassuring, and I wished I had done it earlier. I am certain the results entirely justified the time I took to have a bit of a think.

Think it all through in a blueprint

I learnt this lesson well, and as I started to build my new business, Crazy for Change, I did a lot of thinking and encapsulated everything into a single blueprint for a business that would meet my aspirations.

My blueprint incorporates all my experience, research, professional development and the wisdom of others. It ensures that, like a jigsaw, everything fits together and works seamlessly to achieve my personal and business goals.

My blueprint is not a plan. That comes as a natural consequence of a well-defined blueprint. Think of building a house. The architect will design the building, creating a blueprint describing how every part of the building looks. This blueprint will include all the utilities and connections to achieve what it is supposed to.

It ensures, for instance, that the building will be structurally sound. It includes details such as providing enough electric sockets in each room in the right place and doors that open without colliding with other doors. It incorporates building regulations making sure, for instance, that there are two doors at least between food preparation areas and bathrooms.

It is then up to the builders to plan constructing the building from the blueprint. My blueprint ended up with six sections.

Backstory

You are your business, and its primary purpose is to define what is enough for you and overcome the scarcity in your life. I recall a talk given by Michael Gerber of E-myth fame. Gerber told us that *"your primary role as a business owner is to create more life for yourself"*. Therefore, it should be no surprise that your blueprint starts with you, your story, values, and vision.

Never forget the words of Stephen Covey: *"Begin with the end in mind."* Write down what the end looks like to you.

Strategy

Record the strategies that you intend to follow to give you a competitive advantage. For example, are you going to go for cost leadership, niche targeting, convenience or innovation?

Opting for cost leadership should raise a red flag. This strategy requires enormous resources and can be undermined by your competitor. Furthermore, it leaves you with only one string to your bow. If a competitor undercuts you, you immediately lose your advantage, which is why there can only be one cost leader in a sector.

Your audience

A resilient, long term business will focus on helping clients achieve their aspirations. However, they may need to resolve short term problems in the first place. These could be your way in, as well as providing you with a stepped portfolio of products running from problem to aspiration.

Products

Productise and package everything, even services and marketing assets. It's easier to describe and sell a product than a service.

Think in terms of client commitment as you design your steps, starting with minimal commitment (a little time only) to total commitment (money, time and energy).

Marketing, sales and onboarding

You are now nearly there, and you should be able to join everything together to develop messages, problem and solution trademark phrases, pitches, product packaging, onboarding processes, value propositions, launch runways and publicity. You should be able to extract these from the work you have done in your blueprint. The marvellous thing about the blueprint is that you can make sure everything fits together correctly before going live.

Structure and resources

Describe the corporate structure of your business. For example, will you run as a sole trader, a limited company or a limited liability partnership? Design your exit or succession strategy, and develop a business will to take effect in the event of your premature death or incapacity. Think about money and design initial and projected cash flow and balance sheets. Think about the team you will need to implement your blueprint. You will need to cover marketing, operations and resources at the very least. Paint a picture of how the positions and the people who fill them look. Then draw up position contracts for the roles, and draft employment contracts.

The finishing touches

Remember that this is an important document. Someone who gets hold of it could easily use it to set up a rival business. After all, it's all there. So, ensure it is copyrighted, marked confidential and make clear that distribution and copying are restricted. Your blueprint will evolve. However, it should remain a coherent, structured and complete model of your business which will guide your implementation.

It is an iterative process and is never really finished. The art is to keep going around until everything fits. You will probably start to test markets and messages early on, and as the results come through, you will find it necessary to adjust your blueprint.

Taking time out to have a bit of a think is an essential part of knowing what enough means to you and how you achieve it. Your blueprint is an ideal vehicle for this, so compile it, keep it always at hand and use it as your definitive guide for getting the life you want.

References

(1) Carrol, L (1865).Alice's Adventures in Wonderland. Macmillan, London

(2) Taylor, J (2013).The Chronicles of St Mary's (12 books and 15 short stories). Headline, London. Along with ,And the world went white', this is one of Maxwell's key catchphrases, appearing in many instances in a slightly different form.

About Tricia Van Vleit

Tricia Van Vliet is a licensed Certified Public Accountant in the United States. She is proud to be among tremendous female company as a pioneer of flexible work schedules in a demanding and male-dominated profession. This barrier is one of many broken to honor her dreams as a mom and her career goals. Tricia established herself as a subject matter expert and continues as an industry conference speaker for nearly two decades.

Tricia has audited, coached, and consulted across all U.S. time zones. She started her firm, The Wellness CPA PLLC, to dedicate her accounting career to the real people behind credentials and numbers. In 2020, Tricia reached students virtually as a guest on Kaplan UK Instagram Live COVID-19 series. Her passion for writing and teaching led to developing a college-level course for future accounting professionals, Beyond Balances – Emotional Accounting for a Life-filled Career Journey. Tricia uses this project and others to create space for love, grace, and joy among professionals to save lives threatened by anxiety, depression, and burnout.

Every day, Tricia celebrates her faith and the blessings of her husband, Steve, and their two sons, Cody and Nick.

Meet Tricia at:
https://wellness.cpa
https://www.linkedin.com/in/tricia-van-vliet-cpa-231b9827/
https://www.linkedin.com/company/the-wellness-cpa-pllc/

Patient Courage

Tricia Van Vliet (USA)

*During a perfect and near fatal storm I discovered
a gift I called Patient Courage, with which I am now
re-building my life with meaning and purpose.*

Since I was a little girl playing with dolls, I have never had
dreams or plans that did not include being a mom. I was the
daughter of a devoted stay-at-home mom and wanted to be just
like her.

As a high school and college student, I fell deeply into the message that smart girls should be driven and defined by ambitious
college and career goals. Otherwise, they were compromising.
My dream to be a mom was not worthy of a named goal. So, I
wrote and spoke of goals while keeping my dreams in the silence of my heart. External voices had officially dictated what
was enough.

As it turned out, I was a smart girl who started challenging
the status quo right out of college. My values and personal
dreams led to some very bold moves. I made intentional choices that allowed me to be a mom first and have a successful career in a male-dominated profession. Not the other way around.
I deliberately requested undesirable client assignments when I
knew travel was not required and on-site work was minimal.

At the age of 25, I realized that these assignments were key
to pioneering a flexible work schedule where one did not previous-
ly exist. At my level, billable hours were a crucial metric, and
high-profile clients were the key to advancement. I was willing
to forgo advancement opportunities for the chance to work a
significantly reduced schedule. Most men and many women in

my professional world did not understand. As a result, I was treated like a second-class citizen. Judgment from my peers made it clear that I was not enough.

Ever so subtly, exceeding the ever-moving target of others' expectations was an unspoken baseline that defined my worth. I decided it was a game, and I allowed it to consume me. Desperately, I sought worthiness working in a job that I wanted to love. Unfortunately, my work became barely more than a financial necessity as I lived the dreams of my heart. I was 25, a working mom, and I believed I could beat the game. I decided to gain control over the narrative of expectations. Accordingly, I dictated my own expectations at nothing less than perfection in every aspect of my life to avoid failure personally or professionally. Oh, the stories I told myself with such confidence that I had no choice but to believe.

I was determined to prove that my work mattered and was worthy of respect. Taking my chosen client work in a specialized industry, I used it to become a national-level subject matter expert. With invites to speak at conferences, I quickly earned respect in my profession. Ironically, it was the work that allowed me to be the mom I wanted to be that accelerated my career advancement. I was young and was allowed to work a reduced schedule to be home with my 7- and 3-year-old boys two days per week. I also had an impressive title that warranted a six-figure salary working part-time. Yet somehow, I was still not enough in the eyes of my colleagues. The judgments continued. My time in the office was a blanket of darkness.

Eventually, a firm created a national director position explicitly designed for me. The enticements included the opportunity to be the beta test of the firm's first home office technology package. Other than periodic travel to New York and Chicago, I was home. So began my dream job. I did work that I loved in an emotionally safe place while making lasting friendships. I had escaped the darkness of judgment. The expectations that I set for myself evolved into a seemingly straightforward definition of success based on just two rules. One, be so involved that my family forgets that I have a full-time career. Two, accomplish so much that my firm and colleagues forget that I have a family. It was that simple. I had authored a new game, one of my own. I was certainly on my way to being and having enough.

As years went by, I created incredible opportunities for myself. Technology evolved and was the key to me being the mom I wanted my boys to have. Not only did I never miss my boys' school or sporting events, but I also accepted every opportunity to volunteer at school and church. Likewise, I gave my career as many as 2,600 hours per year. I narrowly survived from one commitment to the next. I did it all (well, minus sleep) until I did nothing.

My refusal to give up on the dreams in my heart and chosen profession translated into a daily, or even hourly, battle with the unreasonable expectations that I set for myself. Eventually, my mind and body could no longer sustain my definition of success. Upon reflection, I had disregarded or fought every warning sign delivered by my body for more than two decades.

Losing my peripheral vision, typing gibberish because my hands were not in sync, ringing in my ears, chronic fatigue, migraines and bronchitis were routine occurrences. Compliance with my rules was not sustainable. I didn't ask for help. Instead, I worked harder to hide the defeat that consumed my heart. In 2015, I ran from public practice into a new national-level job. Beyond a significantly reduced salary, the price tag was my soul. I was doing work plagued with ugly truths that crippled me.

On June 15, 2017, I failed at an attempt to take my own life. My exhaustion and distorted reality led me to believe that I was giving my husband and sons a precious gift. I believed that they would be better off without me. They had been my lifelong dream. The ones I loved more than the air that I breathed. How could I make such a decision for them? How could I have conceived this gift that could have destroyed them? A perceived inability to succeed for my family triggered my actions. My efforts failed that day, and, as a result, I affectionately refer to my attempted suicide as my greatest failure. I believe in celebrating failures. The precious new journey I started that day is something I celebrate every single day.

My greatest failure began a journey to find this woman whom I learned was loved and cherished beyond belief by everyone that mattered. For decades, I drowned in unknowingly created chaos. Ironically, my need for control and refusal to fail led to self-destruction. I lost myself among the roles I played while being everything. Unfortunately, I distorted reality with my assumptions of everything that mattered to everyone who mattered to me. My loving and generous husband patiently helped me to see that. In 2020, we celebrated our 25th wedding anniversary. Simply because when I couldn't breathe, he did for both of us.

With my closest family members, an incredible care team, and a few dear friends, I walked into a brave new life where I care for myself and am vocal about my needs. I ask for help freely. Patient courage is the label I give to the way I approach life's challenges. I believe that I am worthy of love. I choose to love first. Yes, I know that I am enough.

What was once a toxic career has been cleaned and rebuilt with grace-filled expectations. I have a professional life that holds no promise of the certainties I sought in the past. I took a tremendous leap of faith and started my own CPA firm. Each day brings new possibilities for my generous soul because the real human beings behind credentials and numbers come first.

Patient courage compelled me to seek help from others when my heart and technical knowledge were simply insufficient to develop a solid business model. We need human connection. If we keep our heads up with an open mind and heart, we find kind, loving, and generous souls ready to jump in with their skills, knowledge, and experience. Just like people, businesses do not thrive in a vacuum. Patient courage acknowledges that life and business require time and bold steps. Following our calling is worthy of our hearts and money.

My beloved roles as wife, mother, daughter, sister and friend, and the role I enjoy as a professional are no longer mine to balance, but rather I engage them in a beautiful dance each new day. Even if it is with two left feet, my dance is choreographed through love, kindness, and compassion. Patient courage is the melody of my mind. My faith and my core values create the dance floor, or boundaries, that defines my practice.

Patient courage allows me to maintain a healthy lifestyle. I take bold steps for myself and those placed in my life, those that I love and know, and those I call temporary strangers. Temporary strangers are individuals God places in my path unexpectedly and become a part of my story. I see them because I look up from my laptop and task lists to appreciate the beauty of unscripted life.

Patient courage fuels my soul each day with a commitment to share my heart, time, talents and doing the next right thing. Confidently, I walk away from work and personal relationships unaligned with my values. I strive to be a catalyst for change when darkness wants to prevail. With the gift of patient courage, I discern each choice and do my best to offer grace, act with kindness and compassion, and resist judgment for myself and others. These practices are enough on any given day.

Patient courage means that when I am excited or anxious to log in and jump into projects, I choose to breathe and take care of myself first. I begin with prayer, reflection, and gratitude at the start of each new day. Accepting the gifts of a precious new day, exploring what I feel, my blessings, and the sights and sounds of creation. This practice is most effortless when my world bursts with warm fresh air, sunshine, blossoms, and birds singing. It is just as attainable amid silence, cold, and snow.

My prepare for the day routine is done with a pen and my journal. Not only do I feed my passion for writing, but this practice allows me to eliminate distractions. At the same time, I prepare my mind, body, and soul for the new day by waking up my patient courage. Over several months, my journal evolved into a series of distinct and intentional steps. I make it a habit to include my gratitude for the struggles of the last 24 hours. Seemingly counterintuitive, this practice creates space to bravely acknowledge challenges and mistakes that indicate slips back into unhealthy habits of the past.

My prayerful and grateful heart allows me to prioritize my day according to what is personally and professionally essential while protecting my health. My journaling concludes with planning my day. I begin designing the rest of my day with a plan for myself before focusing on my business. Whom do I commit to being today? What actions will demonstrate that commitment? How will I care for myself (hydration, exercise, healthy food choices, and enough sleep) and keep my promises to others? What relationships will I intentionally nurture? Finally, I focus on my CPA firm. Here, my credentials, 25 years of professional experience, and my faith work in concert to create meaningful work. At the same time, my calendar includes standing appointments to fill my water glass and exercise. I am also human and acknowledge the ease with which I can click snooze and eventually dismiss exercise reminders. I am a work in progress and confident that I will ultimately increase my steps beyond those I take to fill my water glass. I offer myself the same grace that I would anyone else that I love.

Patient courage allows me to write my professional love story with a business capable of evolving with the seasons and challenges promised by real life. Day by day, this is enough.

The Next Time You Think You Have Lost It

Tricia Van Vleit (USA)

When I thought that my work had broken me, I spoke these words of defeat to my boys, *"I am sorry, guys, but your mom has lost it."*

Before I could even take a breath, one of them quipped, *"No, mom, you haven't lost it. It's just the bottom of the ninth, and you are down by 10."* In such a small package, such wit and wisdom rewrote my story and turned tears into laughter ... laughter flowing from my mouth and deep within my heart!

Let go of the narrative that says it is all on you and never underestimate the power of human connection.

Speak up and give generous hearts a chance to hear *"I can't do this alone"* even when the only words that come out are, *"I can't do this."*

Be the generous heart that listens and seeks to understand the words spoken by individuals who feel defeated.

You have not lost it, and neither have they.

Be Like the Breeze

Kim LeClair (USA)

you have to keep on going
keep your ideas flowing
if you find you are slowing
hold on to this one knowing
the way through is keep rowing
like the breeze just keep on blowing

New Horizons

Cat Preston (UK) and Caroline Harvey (Spain)

As we have all done, trust that you are enough and have every-thing you need to unlock your own creative potential, make a contribution, connect with others, show that you care and live a life of abundance – in every sense of the word.

If you're reading this chapter, you've reached the end of our collective offering.

First and foremost, we'd like to thank you for giving us your attention and taking your precious time to read our stories. Our greatest hope is that you are left feeling it was time well spent.

Each contribution is the unique and distinctive voice of the talented, heart-centred human who wrote it. Every story contains a powerful message about how to approach – and enter - that liminal space of discovery and in so doing, pursue a purposeful life doing work that matters to you and makes a difference to others.

From the Latin *limen* or threshold, a liminal space is lite-rally crossing over or passing through. A place of transition that often involves leaving behind the safety and security of where we were before, and stepping into the unknown to become someone new. It's a magical place that can bring us face to face with our deepest fears about who we are and how we show up in the world. An opportunity to shed old identities, narratives and beliefs that no longer serve us, and reconnect with our deepest, essential self. It is also a moment when we ask our-selves the questions, *"Am I good enough? Do I know enough? Do I have what it takes to do this?"*

For some, the fear becomes unbearable or paralysing. We remain stuck on the precipice, unable to leap into the void. But for many, thankfully, a threshold is an invitation to surrender control, and trust that on the other side of that fear is a place where we will create something new, and as yet unknown. We learn to dance with fear, find balance and clarity through taking action, and find our own true version of abundance and fulfilment when we are at full integrity with ourselves. We remember how it feels to play and are energised with enthusiasm and the satisfaction of pursuing our dreams.

Life is a journey that takes us through a series of these thresholds. Some we choose, while others present themselves, like a door that's ajar. Each one takes us into the liminal space we must cross to reach that new, uncharted territory.

There is no map. We chart our own path by moving forward with self-compassion, courage and creativity. We take the time we need. Accepting risk, learning from our mistakes, and embracing possibility. There will always be bumps in the road, seemingly insurmountable challenges and periods of self-doubt. As some of these stories attest, it's often our darkest moments that shape us and give us the resilience to carry on.

If we never accept the invitation or take that courageous first step, we may never know what we are capable of and how deep a contribution we can make in the world. The music inside us will remain locked in our hearts forever, and the gift that only we can bring will never be shared.

We are a group of people from different countries, cultures and walks of life. We don't profess to have the perfect solution. What unites us is a desire to make a difference through our work, to connect and contribute through community, and to live in accordance with our values.

What we have each discovered is that there is no perfect way to do things and there are no right answers. We've asked ourselves, "*What if there were no rules?*" thereby giving ourselves permission to craft a life we want to live according to our own inner wisdom – one threshold at a time along a path we have chosen for ourselves. What we have come to understand is that we are better when we work together, use kindness as our compass and celebrate the richness of a diverse world with humility.

As coaches, creatives, teachers, mentors, and leaders from across the globe we have come together to share our stories that have at their heart a simple message: You are enough. Trust that you have everything you need to take that first step and unlock your own creative potential to make a contribution, connect with others, show that you care and live a life of abundance – in every sense of the word.

We leave you with words of the great writer, poet and inspirational sage, Maya Angelou:

"*We need much less than we think we need.*"

Don't wait for our permission. The key is right there in your hand.

Steps

Kim LeClair (USA)

Sometimes a small step
seems like standing still.
Sometimes standing still
seems like a great step.

Acknowledgements

A Collaborative Project

You are able to read this book because sixteen people from around the world got together to share their stories, wisdom and skills. We have worked together to write, set and publish this book ourselves, excepting only the appointment of Siobhan Curham, an external professional editor, to check and comment on the penultimate draft. We are indebted to her for her expertise, care and formidable attention to detail. This book is undoubtedly better because of her input and we are so grateful to her for the invaluable role she played as a guide and mentor. We are so lucky to have you as part of our team.

Special thanks to Ulla Raaf for the beautiful cover and interior design and for the painstaking work of type-setting our work. Her patience, dedication and creativity have been a real gift in bringing this book to life.

We thank the many friends and family who have helped with the support, encouragement and precious feedback that has made all of this possible. From gracious and supportive reviews to just simply being there to listen and reminding us what really matters, we appreciate you all.

This book is, therefore, a testament to the power of collaboration. We split into three teams as follows:

The Editorial Team: Jeremy Deedes, Ian Berry, Caroline Harvey, Cat Preston

The Publication Team: Ulla Raaf (including complete design), Ian Berry, Claudia Brose, Jeremy Deedes

The Promotions Team: Jackie Davis, Claudia Brose, Joel Hughes (mailing list), Kim LeClair (website), Darcy Lee, Cat Preston (podcast), Ulla Raaf

If you would like to hear us talking about our project and the work we do you can listen to episode 41 of The Collective Wisdom Podcast with Cat Preston

the Right Company

the **Right Company** supports a caring cohort of business owners, freelancers and creative solopreneurs, to create the career or company that serves them as well as their customers. People like you, who want to build a viable business they're proud of and who want to do work that brings them joy. If you want **a business that's right for you**, you need to be in ... *the* **Right Company**.

You can find *the* **Right Company** at https://therightcompany.co

Keeping in touch

And finally, our thanks must go to you, the reader, for gifting us with your attention. If you have found anything helpful within these pages, it is our hope that you will share your insight and help us reach more people by leaving a review or reaching out to us at https://enoughthebook.co/

May you enjoy a sense of **enoughness** in your life.

Lightning Source UK Ltd.
Milton Keynes UK
UKHW010825251121
394585UK00011B/772